Sally's mental health colleag

I have known Sally for many years and v sionate about her work, especially in the area of s to commit to their change and reach their perate from a place of integrity, passion and su
Dorothy Denis Executive Coach and C
uk.linkedin.com/in/dorothydenis

I highly recommend Sally Baker. She is insightful, experienced and a genuinely amazing woman whom I am blessed to have work with myself. Her ethical approaches are excellent and I could not recommend her enough. Thank you, Sally, for being exactly who you are.
Vonnie Crosbie Ayanay Psychological Accreditation
www.ayanay.co.uk

Sally is a caring, inspirational intelligent, brilliant and highly effective therapist, truly knowledgable in her field and I am very proud to know and endorse her.
Tim Phizackerley PTSD & Trauma specialist
www.ptsd-specialist.co.uk

As the associate therapist at The Hunt Academy for Young Actors, Sally has been a godsend. Her work with our young actors, either through her mental health management workshops or through her much needed 1:1s for young people that may be struggling, has transformed our ability as an academy to give a "whole person" approach to actor training. Many of our young actors, following Sally's interventions, have gone on to achieve in ways they couldn't have dreamt of prior to working with her. Sally Baker really has exceptional skills for unlocking human potential.
Sarah Hunt Academy Director, HAYA
www.thehuntacademy.co.uk

I have known Sally Baker for several years and she is an experienced international therapist, author of excellent self-development books, an inspiring motivational speaker, a blogger and a social media commentator. Sally brings her natural warmth, empathy, sensitivity, humour and clarity to all her work. She encourages others to change unhelpful habits from the past, process disturbing emotions and find hope with happiness for the future.
Keith Chadwick
www.cbt-centre.co.uk

Sally is a master of the human mind as well as the human heart. She knows how to keep you engrossed and engaged at every turn. If you want to build your resilience, you'll, find no better guide.
April Adams Emotional Health Consultant
www.AprilAdams.org

Sally is one of my favourite people. As a colleague she has always been a sage adviser to me in times of emotional difficulty (which have been many over the years!). I have had the privilege of hearing about her transformational work, particularly with her use of Orpheus technology, and this book is a must-read for anyone looking to build their resilience.
Dr David Jay Chief Executive Officer
orpheusmindtechnologies.com

I've known Sally Baker as a friend and trusted colleague for many years. She's a fantastic, highly skilled therapist and the first person I call if I want a second opinion.
Steve Blampied
www.themindfixer.com

I was a regular co-contributor with Sally on a radio program that explored the devastating effects on the lives of survivors of childhood sexual abuse. Sally spoke with conviction and frequently evidenced her professional experience and how working with clients with trauma and PTSD informed with her lived experience.
Chris Tuck Trauma-Informed Health & Wellness Coach, Lived Experience Activist/ Campaigner re CSA/E
www.christuckmotivationalspeakerandtrainer.co.uk

I've known Sally for almost 25 years. We've ran therapy groups together; written books together and mutually supported each other in our work as therapists. I trust her implicitly and hold her in the highest regard.
Liz Hogon Therapy Specialist in Emetophobia
www.Lizhogon.com

Sally is the embodiment of integrity and resilience in her personal and professional life. She is passionate about, and dedicated to, her work and her clients. Sally draws on a wealth of lived and professional experience in helping others achieve their true potential. She has been an insightful and generous mentor to me in my Psychotherapy Masters training.
Lizzie Henson Pluralistic Psychotherapist (MSc) in training

I really value Sally's professional input and wonderful common sense. I met Sally before lockdown and she was a constant support and friendship throughout an extremely difficult time for us all. Huge congratulations on your book Sally – a well-deserved achievement.
Bernie Wright NEDDE Training, Co-Director, Neurodiversity, Eating Disorders & Distressed Eating
www.neddetraining.co.uk

The Getting of Resilience from the inside out

Sally Baker

Foreword by

Andy Wasley, journalist and RAF veteran

Hammersmith Health Books
London, UK

First published in 2024 by Hammersmith Health Books – an imprint of
Hammersmith Books Limited
4/4A Bloomsbury Square, London WC1A 2RP, UK
www.hammersmithbooks.co.uk

Disclaimer: The educational content provided here is for informational purposes only and is not a substitute for professional medical or mental health advice, diagnosis or treatment. The information contained herein is not intended to treat, diagnose or provide specific recommendations for any individual and should not be used as such. The techniques and coping methods discussed are not meant to be comprehensive or apply to every situation. You should consult directly with your own physician or mental health provider regarding any emotional, psychological or medical concerns prior to trying any self-help recommendations.

Any testimonials or opinions expressed by contributors represent their personal experiences and do not indicate endorsement by the publisher or creators of this content. We make no guarantees regarding the accuracy or applicability of this content for any individual's specific needs. Ultimately, you assume full responsibility for the choices and application of any ideas contained herein.

A note on confidentiality: Case studies included here are grounded in the author's clinical experience. She has, however, taken all possible precautions to disguise individuals' identity. Occasionally a case study is a composite of experiences from several different clients who presented with similar challenges so that any one individual client is unidentifiable.

British Library Cataloguing in Publication Data: a CIP record of this book is available from the British Library.

Print ISBN: 978-1-78161-126-5
Ebook ISBN: 978-1-78161-127-2

Commissioning editor: Georgina Bentliff
Front cover design: Annie Rickard Straus
Text designed and typeset by: Julie Bennett of Bespoke Publishing Ltd
Index: Dr Laurence Errington
Production: Angela Young
Printed and bound by: TJ Books Limited, Cornwall UK

Contents

More than education, more than experience, more than training, a person's level of resilience will determine who succeeds and who fails. That's true in the cancer ward, it's true in the Olympics and it's true in the boardroom.

Dean Becker, *CEO, Adaptiv Learning Systems, 2002*

Foreword

An anecdote.

It's a bitterly cold February morning. In watery pre-dawn light, I stand by a dark copse of snow-dusted pines on a bleak Northumberland moor. Either side of me, clad in camouflage, my fellow Royal Air Force officer cadets shiver as the icy wind stirs up swirls of snowflakes.

'A man's a man, for a' that…' A cadet stands in front of us, reading Robert Burns's poem aloud. The words do little to stir the soul. Soon we'll embark on the toughest physical and mental leadership exercise of our six-month training course: a brutal slog around the training area, exercising our intellect, leadership skills and physical endurance. A test, above all, of our resilience. I'm 19, uncertain, painfully immature, and have tried and failed to pass this test already. This is my last chance.

Resilience can mean many things. That morning in Northumberland, it was all about being able to keep body, mind and spirit functioning under assault from the elements and the weight of expectation. Success meant a good chance to secure the career we were all striving for. For me, it also meant freedom from a broken family and trauma. Something kept me going, despite crippling self-doubt and physical exhaustion. That 'something' was resilience.

My memory of that morning is so vivid I can all but feel the wintry breeze. I'm sure you have a similar memory, of some moment of reckoning that tested your resilience to its limits, and forever altered your sense of self. I have had many such moments, in my personal and professional life: first, as someone living with the consequences of childhood abuse and trauma; then, in my careers in the RAF and as a journalist working across news and travel.

What I've learned from those moments is that resilience is a skill that can be learned and practised, even if it occasionally requires an extraordinary degree of self-awareness and emotional intelligence. As this book will demonstrate, even those characteristics can be developed if you can be mindful, pragmatic and – above all – compassionate.

I grew up in a broken home, enduring the stresses that any child experiences when their parents hurtle towards divorce. My mother was physically and emotionally abusive, regularly subjecting me to pain, fear, humiliation and isolation. My father – compassionate, loving and supportive – suffered under appalling stress arising from unemployment and our disintegrating family: I was with him when he suffered the heart attack that left him unable to care for me for most of my adolescence. I found myself forced to survive in my mother's home, living with her unpredictable rages and abusive behaviour – and witnessing the stress and danger she faced at the hands of my mentally unstable stepfather.

I had another challenge: I was a young gay man, growing up in a society where it was still acceptable for mass media to stoke moral panics about LGBT+ people. Section 28, a vindictive law preventing the 'promotion' of homosexuality by public bodies, meant teachers did little to address the homophobic bullying I faced at school. The very idea of falling in love and living a full and happy life seemed absurd.

These were heavy burdens for a young man to carry, and I still feel their weight. I have struggled with my mental health, and been diagnosed with attention-deficit hyperactivity disorder (ADHD), a condition that is especially likely to be expressed in people who experience childhood trauma. Years of therapy and medical treatment have helped me to understand the deep impact of trauma and ADHD on my life, and to improve my ability to cope with difficult times.

For all that, when I look back on my childhood and consider its lifelong impact I do so without anger or regret: rather, I see it as an apprenticeship in resilience. Without realising it, through those difficult years I learned about the one thing that I think forms the foundation for resilience: compassion.

I was very lucky to have a father who made huge sacrifices to support me. I was a flinty, angry and self-absorbed teenager, dealing with appalling mental stresses and the growing academic and emotional costs of unrecognised ADHD. My father's patience never faltered: he championed my creativity, celebrated my achievements and provided me with as much stability as his reduced circumstances would allow. His compassion sustained me through those long and difficult years. It still does.

Compassion fuelled my resilience through adult life too. The RAF became a surrogate family of sorts; when I suffered from depression and anxiety, my colleagues embraced me and championed me. When I lived through the challenges of active service, as we all did – rocket attacks in Afghanistan, vigils and funerals for fallen friends, the demands of humanitarian service – our mutual support, kindness and compassion played a far greater role in keeping us all going than any notion of 'toughness' or 'masculinity'.

It can be hard to receive compassion, or to acknowledge a need for it, in a society that values a stiff upper lip. Even harder, sometimes, is the challenge of self-compassion, which loses out easily to shame and regret. My shame springs from the traumas of childhood abuse and growing up gay in an era of state-sponsored homophobia. It's boosted by the struggles I face due to ADHD – emotional dysfunction, professional failure, broken relationships and a deep sense of incapability. Self-compassion tells me I have done well in life despite those challenges, and helps me to find the will to persevere. Without it, my resilience falters and I struggle to keep going.

Compassion, of course, can flow two ways. Showing compassion can be just as valuable as receiving it in building up our resilience. The Mental Health Foundation reports that people can experience mental health benefits when they are kind to other people. Acts of kindness can even activate a 'helper's high', making us feel better physically and mentally.

Certainly, my own experiences with compassion, both offered and received, convince me it is the key to my resilience. I've hugged civilians who had lost everything in a devastating hurricane; been comforted by strangers when I've suffered from bereavement or trauma; and learned to find compassion for myself when I've felt useless or alone. It helps to know that each episode of compassion has added to my store of resilience, enabling me to face challenges I can't foresee and to engage with past traumas in a healthy and self-fulfilling way.

That morning in Northumberland, I couldn't shake off the fear and shame I'd carried into the RAF from my childhood. Now, I can look back on that 19-year-old cadet and feel proud of his resilience – because it made me who I am. You deserve the chance to build up your resilience and be your best self too – and you will find a good companion in these pages.

Sally Baker has a lifetime's experience of offering people practical ways to build resilience into their lives. Through her therapeutic practice, she has helped people in appalling distress to find the means to be kind to themselves. Her act of compassion is to offer this guidance to you now. In these pages you'll find solace and encouragement and, I hope, the understanding that resilience isn't something intrinsic and unchangeable; you can develop it, and learn to face life's challenges with greater resolve and confidence.

Whether you're facing strains at work or at home, or looking out for a friend or relative, this is a book that will forever change the way you look at life and its difficulties. If you came to this book feeling cheerful, I hope it gives you more reasons to smile. But if it's open now because you're struggling, be assured that in Sally's words you'll find reasons to look ahead to brighter days.

Andy Wasley
Journalist and RAF veteran

About the author

Sally Baker's therapeutic approach is integrative, drawing on a range of theories and techniques, including Emotional Freedom Technique (EFT), Humanistic Therapy, Brainwave Recursive Therapy (BWRT) and Neurolinguistic Programming (NLP) -based approaches. She puts a high value on having a collaborative relationship between therapist and client and adapts her approach to meet the unique needs and goals of each individual.

As a clinical supervisor, Sally provides support and guidance for other therapists to ensure they are providing the best possible care for their clients. She is also an experienced writer and has appeared in various media outlets discussing mental health topics.

Sally believes that everyone has the ability to improve their mental health and wellbeing and is committed to helping people live happier, more fulfilling lives. She is passionate about breaking down the stigma surrounding mental health problems and promoting the importance of seeking help when needed.

Acknowledgements

I am grateful for the love and forbearance of my husband, the painter Arnold Dobbs. I am grateful for being loved and included in four generations of his extended family. I am grateful for my son Eliot Oswald-Baker and his wife Sarah who I humbly watch raising their son Jarvis with great kindness and care. I am grateful for the Irish wing of my family and the care and love they give me without a moment's hesitation. Makes me feel blessed.

I am grateful for my long-time friend and wise mentor, the Melbourne-based therapist Liz Hogon, with whom I co-wrote my first two books. I value her in-depth knowledge and inspiration as well as her unfailing generosity, encouragement and love. I am also grateful for the open dialogue with my professional colleagues working daily with clients struggling with complex mental health issues, especially the support of Siobhan, Bernie and Lizzie.

I am grateful for my friend and PR Manager, Carrie Eddins, for her expertise and unerring faith in me with her 'Why not you?' mantra, reminding me not to play small. She regularly has me head-hunted for guest television appearances and expert comments in the media on human behaviour the world over.

This book was a long time in the writing, longer than I or anyone else thought or had initially hoped. I would like to thank my publisher, Georgina Bentliff, for her continuing faith and forbearance, especially at times when I faltered.

My story

My family background makes me think about all the things I am versus all the things I am not. One way to illustrate this is with my name: Sally Baker. I was born Sally Baker to a father named Harry Baker or Henry Jackson. He was born either in 1912 or 1914. He was the same man who just happened to have two names and two dates of birth on two different birth certificates. Over one hundred years ago, during the Edwardian period, confusion over family lineage was not unusual in the working class. So, although, in theory, there was a 50:50 chance of my being called Sally Jackson, I grew up oblivious to that possibility for a long time as Sally Baker.

In the Baker family, ambition was not encouraged. My mum took books away from me as I was growing up. She said I spent too much time reading and that nothing good ever happened to a girl who knew too much. Hey, who knew? I recall my father often telling the teenage me that what would make him proud was if I trained and qualified as a nurse. Note not a doctor, as that would have been unthinkable. He had me pegged to be a nurse, and that was that. (That is not to say that being a nurse is not a worthy ambition; it is an exceedingly tough training and of course much more professional and based on scientific knowledge now than it was when I was growing up. It was the lack of 'either/or' that was so limiting.) But what hurt me the most was his lack of stretch and the lack of aspiration for me. The fact he didn't aspire for me to be a doctor made me believe there was something unworthy about me.

So, parental ambition to succeed at all costs wasn't my pressure. I felt the inverse pressure from a lack of expectation that my parents had vested in me.

As it happens, this has been one of the most challenging subjects I've attempted to write about. Childhood trauma may require a lifetime's vigilance to know how those experiences can undermine resilience building. The whole process of researching the latest thinking about resilience effectively highlighted where my old negative self-judgements lurked and where my lingering self-sabotaging habits hid.

Like many others, I've been challenged with 'the getting of resilience' for myself. I have had to find my way through the tangled web of negative feelings I developed growing up, including limiting beliefs I took into adulthood. I had also developed entrenched beliefs that I was never good enough or worthy of happiness. I'm a prime example of how growing up, even in a functioning and loving family, doesn't always protect one from the outside world.

My seven-year-old self's world fell apart when I was sexually assaulted by two teenage brothers who were the sons of friends of my family. There's an old-school photograph of me in a summer dress, looking directly at the camera. When I look at that image of me, I try hard to determine whether this is a before or after picture. I still acknowledge that sexual assault changed my perception of myself and how I understood my place in the world.

In retelling this story, like many survivors of abuse, ingrained minute details of what happened are still vivid in my memory. Ask me which day of the week or year, and I'd struggle to be accurate. But everything I've written here is true. That kind of disparity typically double-binds abuse survivors in law courts and stops them from being recognised as reliable witnesses.

These family friends were unlike any other friends of my parents. My Dad felt an old allegiance to stay in touch with the boys' father as they had fought in the same regiment in the Second World War. My dad's friend had been disabled in conflict and had barely been able to work since he was de-mobbed. They were conspicuously poor in many ways. Their home looked make-shift, with a collapsed sofa, old curtains as throws over the armchairs, and the furniture worn and mismatched. Looking back, we visited them two or three times a year and probably neither my father nor mother wanted to, but it had become an expectation on both sides.

On one of these Sunday afternoon visits, the elder boy, who was around 17 or 18 years old, asked me to ride with him on his new motorbike. My mom categorically said no, but I must have bugged and annoyed her until, in a fit of peak, she said, 'Oh, go on but stay on this road and come straight back.' He took me to the rear of the house, where an old utility room had been roughly converted into a workshop with a workbench under the window. The room was littered with engine parts from motorbikes and cars. It smelt of oil and dust.

Once I was separated from my family, he acted quickly. I can't remember if the motorbike ride ever happened. I can remember being lifted onto the workbench and his slightly younger brother holding me down as they sexually assaulted me. It could have been hours, but it was minutes. The older one spoke close into my ear so that I could feel his breath. He said this was what I'd wanted, and it was our secret.

I was mute and frozen in fear. My mum had gone to the front door to look out for me on the older boy's motorbike, and when she couldn't see us on the road, she began walking through the house, calling my name. She had interrupted them, and they lifted me back down from the workbench onto my feet and pushed me towards the door just as my mum appeared. She looked at the two young men and pulled me by my wrist. She was angry and confused about why I was in that room with them, but nothing else was said. I remember her saying I should stay by her side for the rest of the visit. I remember standing still and silent beside the over-stuffed armchair where she sat chatting with the adults. When I caught her eye, she looked away, obviously angry with me.

The incident was only referred to weeks later on one Saturday afternoon. I was in the living room while my mum finished some decorating. I remember her standing on a pair of step ladders when she casually announced that we would visit that family again the next day.

My bottled-up and unexpressed fear must have gushed out of me as I began to sob loudly. I felt inconsolable, almost unable to breathe, gagging with hysteria at the thought of returning to that house and those men. I remember my mother rushing down the step ladder and trying to contain my thrashing arms as she held onto me, trying to quiet and comfort me. She knew now that something had happened that day. In a raised, urgent voice, she asked, 'What did they do to you? What did they do?'

I can't picture what words I used to describe the assault. I was seven years old. I knew nothing other than the language of Mum and Dad's tickles and hugs. I don't think I even had a name for my vagina, but without words, my mother still understood. I know she held me for a long time. I know that she cried with me, and then she sharply held me away from her at arm's length and ordered me, 'Do not tell your father!' At that moment, I told myself that it was because this had been my mistake and was my shame to bear alone.

My story perfectly illustrates how bad things can happen to anyone, but it's the story we tell ourselves about those events that can cause the most harm. My mother must have dried my tears and told me to forget what had happened. She then said when we went to their house the next day, I was to stay close to her and not move out of her sight. I protested and cried bitterly, but the visit went ahead as planned. I remember how on that visit and many subsequent visits, I would stand by that same over-stuffed, collapsing armchair by my mother's side and neither speak nor move until it was time to leave and return home again.

I created more of my story from being made to go on those visits. I told myself a dark tale about how no one cared about me and that I was just to be compliant and quiet. The judgements I made about myself at the age of seven were to colour my life for decades as the story I continued to tell myself played out in my actions and responses to reinforce my belief that I was shameful and to blame for everything wrong that happened to me. I can remember being that child and feeling that I wasn't safe. It made me in such a rush to grow up. It was as if I'd discovered how dangerous it was to be small and wordless.

The sexual assault wasn't spoken of again for almost 30 years, and much had happened by then. At just 17, I went to live with my much older boyfriend in Exeter, Devon. Although my mother and father tried to legally stop me from leaving home, the social worker they were appointed said it was too late to intervene as the family relationship had broken down. She said I'd probably run away if I were made a Ward of the Court.

Growing up, I habitually put my safety at risk with men I barely knew. In my mind, I toyed with imaginary headlines in tabloid newspapers that read 'Girl Found Dead in a Ditch', believing it was only a matter of time until it came true. In my mind, I almost wanted to fulfil the prophecy that it was all my fault and I was to blame – the very same story I'd been telling myself all those years.

It nearly did come true a year after I moved to Devon, and I was abducted and raped by a stranger. Falling into conversation with him as I walked home enjoying the afternoon sun, I foolhardily agreed to join him for a drink at a local pub we knew was five minutes' walk further along the road. He said his car was right there, and I was surprised by his insistence on driving as the pub was so close. As soon as the car doors closed, his behaviour changed in a blink of an eye from someone seemingly friendly and harmless to an ominously silent and cold stranger. In a moment or two, he drove past the pub and out of Exeter City into the countryside, eventually stopping at a car park along the headland at Exmouth on the coast. I was gone for over six hours before he dumped me at a bus stop with my clothes torn and dishevelled.

By age 35, I had a five-year-old son and had just left my first husband after seven turbulent years of marriage. By then, my mother and I had built bridges back to each other. Our mutual need for reconnection was made even more poignant by the birth of my son sadly coinciding, within a couple of weeks, with of the death of my beloved father.

A family conference was called to discuss what my options were on leaving my husband. My elder brother and his wife hosted the meeting to discuss my future. Mine was the first divorce in our extended family and, although some of my cousins, nieces and nephews followed suit over the years, I was uncomfortably blazing this particular trail. My mother made her feelings known after dinner. She said I'd made a dreadful mistake and had to bear the consequences; as far as she was concerned, my independent life was over; I should return home to the Midlands and live with her and raise my son there. I was equally adamant that I wanted to continue to live and work in London.

We began to clear the dining table after talking late into the night. My brother said out loud, almost as an aside and certainly not to anyone in particular, a thought he'd just had. He said, 'Well, I know this is a difficult time for Sally and her son, but as a family, we can honestly say we've been lucky, and nothing terrible has ever happened to us.' I caught my mother's eye as she quickly looked down. I heard myself saying as if I was far away, 'That's not true, is it, Mum?'

She sat slowly down at the table again, looked at me with tears streaming down her face, and said, 'I thought you would have forgotten about that. You were so young.' I told her I remembered it clearly in every last detail, and her sobs wracked her whole body on hearing me. My brother and his wife were both shocked and confused. I drew up a chair next to my mother's at the table, and it was as if every other person in the room faded out of our perception. It was almost as though every item in the dining room faded too, until the walls faded and the house faded, and my mum and I were just there alone, crying together for that little girl. It felt like an age before my mum could speak and get her words out. She told me she had returned to that house on the bus the next day. She said she had waited out of sight around the corner from their street until her friends had left together to go shopping. Mum knew the two boys would be in the house as neither worked.

She said she had hammered on the front door for ages and, for a moment or two, thought she wouldn't be able to wake them until the elder son came to the door looking grumpy and stale with sleep. She told me she had threatened him with the police. She had threatened him with everything she could think of. She had sworn she'd kill him and his brother if they touched me again. She told me she had made herself hoarse from shouting at him and caused so much commotion on the front step that his younger brother eventually came to the door, too, and she had repeated all her threats.

I was aghast. I was so proud of my mother for speaking out for me, but I was also immeasurably sad. 'Oh Mum, why didn't you tell me you'd been to see them? I thought you were angry at me, and it was all my fault.' She said she had thought that if she never mentioned it to me again, I would forget about it, and everything could return to normal. I asked her why I wasn't to tell my father and if it had been because he wouldn't love me. She answered that she had been frightened that if he had known what they had done to me, he would have gone to their house to have it out with them. She said she knew they were sly and strong. She was worried they would fight with my much older father and they would hurt him or worse, so she was trying to protect him too. She explained that we had to maintain the visits so my dad wouldn't suspect anything was awry.

It had taken almost 30 years to process the story I had told myself. It was never my fault and never my shame. As young and ill-equipped as I was to describe what had happened, I had been heard. My mother's mistake had been to omit ever calling me to her side to reassure me that she'd stood up for me, had spoken out for me, and that I was okay.

The story I had told myself caused me harm for a long time, and I spent many years dealing with the fallout of the negative judgements I made about myself from what had happened to me and how I believed my mother blamed me. I've come a long way with resolving and letting go of my limiting beliefs and recognising my self-doubt. However, I've discovered there's nothing quite like writing a book on resilience to make me question my assumptions and highlight my vulnerabilities all over again.

1. Introduction: The need for resilience

Life-changing events can happen anywhere. As a therapist who works online and in-person, my clients come from around the world. I've listened to voices from almost every continent and heard stories from those who live just a short train ride away. Although each client's story is unique, I've found a common thread that often begins in childhood.

People typically come to therapy to resolve issues like anxiety, panic attacks or depression. However, my long-term interest is in working with those who struggle with self-sabotaging behaviours and limiting beliefs that originated when they felt powerless as children.

Through therapeutic techniques, clients discover their negative self-judgements began when young and didn't comprehend situations fully. They may have wrongly assumed guilt or shame. Many subconsciously decided they didn't deserve happiness or success, so they undermined themselves. This manifests as addictions or self-harm, but also in emotional eating, workaholism, overspending, hoarding or poor money management.

Everyone faces adversity, and sometimes there is little we can do to prevent harm. However, research shows the judgements people make about those events often cause the most enduring damage.

When young, we make sense of negative events through an incomplete worldview. With limited resources, children may wrongly blame themselves, incorporating shame and self-blame into their identity. This colours choices for decades.

While each story differs, a common thread for many clients is an inner scared, isolated child who desperately seeks love and acceptance. To get those needs met, people may use addictions or poor choices to distract from feeling empty inside. The most powerful intervention helps clients authentically accept themselves. With courage, years of self-hate can transform into self-love through therapy.

Examining resilience reveals popular definitions are inaccurate. We shouldn't expect to easily overcome any hardship. Challenges make everyone feel vulnerable. However, some find inner strength like magic. Resilience varies based on how childhood and family dynamics encouraged helpful or harmful thought patterns about oneself.

This book examines how the family you grew up in can impact your ability to develop resilience. It shares therapy tools to develop resilience, so you can trust yourself through adversity. With simple steps, you can change unhelpful thoughts and behaviours learned when young. The aim is to build resilience for life's challenges.

Bad things happen

A unifying theme of all my work is that negative things happen to pretty much everyone and, of course, there are often times when there is little anyone can do to stop bad things from happening. The repercussions of those adverse events and the direct harm people experience can be considerable. It is, however, often the judgement a person makes about themselves in relation to those events that can go on to cause them the most significant and enduring long-term harm.

Negative self-judgements are often made from these adverse events when a person is very young, and are processed emotionally through an incomplete worldview. With limited resources and immature comprehension, young people may well internalise events and wrongly blame themselves. Misappropriated self-blame and shame become a part of how they think and feel about themselves and can colour their choices, behaviours and decisions for decades.

Just as one might expect, everyone's story is unique. When a person seeks out someone like me, a therapist, to help them make sense of their life, they share their circumstances, which embody a broad spectrum of situations, memories and events. However, they often get caught up more in their own story than exploring and focusing on how they responded to their experience.

Having worked with thousands of clients over the years and listened as they shared their stories, I have grown increasingly aware of similarities in experiences, ways of thinking and even behaviour. A sort of common thread or universal human truth has evolved for me and it is this. It is not what happens to a person in their life that ultimately matters; it is the judgements they tell themselves about those events that will aid their ability to bounce back or leave them stuck, stumbling and bloodied. I've come to recognise this variable as resilience. And that's the thing about resilience: you might not call it that or even know the role it plays in your life, but the concept shows up, hidden in plain sight, influencing all of the responses to whatever life throws in your path.

A human commonality

My clients who share their hearts and minds with me, whatever their presenting issue, frequently have one thing in common. It is that, inside almost every one of them, is a scared and isolated child, terrified of being alone and desperate to be loved and accepted. For many, everything they say or do is to satisfy that need.

Ideally, resilience is created in childhood out of the experience of feeling loved and accepted; those raised in ways that did not encourage the development of healthy self-esteem often search for love and acceptance externally to themselves. They can find substitutes such as addictive behaviour, including comfort eating or drugs or alcohol. They frequently do anything to distract themselves, even temporarily, from the void they feel inside. Or, they make questionable life choices that sabotage their ability to thrive and fulfil their true potential.

The most enduring way to heal the inner child and transform how anyone thinks and feels about themselves is to give them what their heart desires – to feel authentic love and acceptance for who they are.

Freedom from emotional pain arising from the worst of times can be achieved by trusting the therapeutic process. It takes courage to turn years of self-hate and well-practised negative self-talk into authentic self-acceptance and love, but it is a crucial step in making peace with oneself and one's past, and it can be done.

And that is the work.

Common misconceptions about resilience

Taking a closer look at resilience, it is clear that several interpretations of the word and many of the popular definitions aren't helpful or accurate. The idea that we should all 'be resilient' and overcome any new challenges with ease and fortitude, whatever they are, isn't valid. We naturally feel vulnerable and unsure of ourselves in the face of hardship and adversity.

When faced with a challenging time, you might know someone who seemed to access some inner strength, almost like a magical internal source of power, that helped them pull through. An example could be when an under-prepared amateur runs a marathon and struggles towards the finish line despite being exhausted. You can also see it when some people face an unexpected health crisis. With the odds stacked against them, they find the emotional reserves to move themselves towards recovery.

The extent to which you can overcome adversities is not determined simply by luck, personality traits or some subjective concept of having the 'right' character. So, how do some people access their inner strength or resilience when needed, and other people struggle with feeling overwhelmed and out of control? To a large degree, your responses are predetermined by several factors, often beyond your control, including how you were raised as a child and the family dynamic you experienced. I look at the role of the family in the up-and-coming chapter called 'The family and other players', exploring some of the critical family dynamics that can encourage unhelpful ways of thinking about oneself that can undermine your ability to develop resilience.

The very nature of resilience is that not everyone has it to call upon. Each person has a unique way of facing and interpreting the world. In the mind of the resilient person, they automatically have a conviction that allows them to find meaning in any challenge they face. Instead of experiencing feelings of being overwhelmed, they are quickly able to adapt to whatever situation occurs and shift to plan B, or even plan X, Y or Z, for that matter. They come up with solutions almost out of thin air. They do all of this while others do not.

The opposite happens in the mind of a person with an underdeveloped sense of resilience. The ability to be adaptive and responsive to different circumstances can feel very challenging. Changes and unexpected events can make a person feel like the world has suddenly switched to Mandarin Chinese, and all understanding and ability are lost.

It's worth bearing in mind that resilience is also not a case of 'having resilience or not'. Resilience is a spectrum response, often stronger or weaker in different areas of your life. For instance, many people feel more resilient in their work and less resilient in their relationships. In therapy, I call these different ways of thinking and feeling about yourself as being defined by arenas. For instance, people with low self-esteem often excel in their work. When properly organised and run fairly, work generally operates within a recognised structure with principles about how people should behave and speak to each other. The rules of work, either formal or implied, provide a paradigm, a system which offers clarity, and when you do well, your efforts are acknowledged and even rewarded.

Sport is another arena that works to increase self-esteem. Again, team or solo sports offer validation of achievement can provide respite and a boost if you often feel beleaguered and lost.

What we learnt about resilience in the time of Covid

The global Covid-19 pandemic was in full swing when I started researching this book. Here in the United Kingdom, we held our breath and braced ourselves for the impact of the double-whammy of an encroaching winter and the forecast second wave of the virus. At that point, it was impossible to foresee how the pandemic would play out nationally and throughout the world over the next few years. The ongoing uncertainty inevitably took its toll, making the situation difficult for everyone. Many people struggled with increased anxiety and stress and found themselves unable to sleep or focus as well as they used to.

It's no surprise that psychologists already acknowledge that living for an extended period of time with chronic stress, such as a pandemic, can harm people's mental health, yet not everyone experienced the same emotional fall-out from those real-life stressors. For some people, the feelings of being overwhelmed coupled with a loss of autonomy because of the imposition of Covid-19 restrictions, plunged them back into their old, familiar feelings of powerlessness they had experienced in childhood. Many people may not have initially made a conscious connection between their youth and their feelings about Covid-19. Still, clients showed up in their droves for therapy feeling fearful, with heightened anxiety levels. When I explored a client's anxiety, it became clear that, like the layers of an onion, at its heart were unresolved emotional challenges from childhood making it more difficult, or even impossible, to manage the negative emotions triggered by the unprecedented challenges of a pandemic.

During this same period, other people successfully managed the practical and emotional turmoil of lockdown and adapted to the restrictions imposed on how they lived and worked. This latter group exhibited signs of feeling more emotionally robust and better able to flourish at times, even when the circumstances were not their choice.

Same boat, different storm

The reasons for the spectrum of responses to the hardships of the pandemic were, of course, complex. However, according to the media, this was supposedly a collective experience, and we were all in the same boat. But, to keep the metaphor going, some people's boats were akin to well-equipped ocean-going liners while other people felt as though they were adrift in a barely water-tight dinghy that threatened to take on water. The pandemic experience may have been universal, but how you responded to it was deeply personal and individual.

Your ability to hunker down and dig deep into your emotional resources during the pandemic was foretold to a large degree. To be able to respond in a resourceful way, a few key markers would have indicated if your abilities were hampered or improved — for instance, the ability to recall previous successful coping strategies. We know the pandemic was unprecedented, so you had never faced the entirety of this challenge before but being able to remember facing other difficulties in the past and how you overcame them could well have been crucial in deciding the ease with which you faced the pandemic versus the depth of suffering you experienced from anxiety, depression and other negative emotions.

Human connection is key

Another marker that would indicate some people could maintain emotional balance while living through those unprecedented times was feeling emotionally supported. Interestingly, adequate emotional support wasn't dependent on proximity for it to be advantageous. It certainly didn't mean that those living alone were automatically at a disadvantage compared to those living in households. Many people living in busy families reported that they were just as prone to feelings of loneliness as those who physically lived alone. However, what made the difference was the quality of human connection to friends and family members, where individuals felt heard and valued. This provided a sense of succour and support even over great geographical distances.

Emotional life-lines came from surprising sources in those unusual circumstances. The simple kindness and care of other adults, neighbours and friends helped to build self-esteem and self-reliance. People believed more in themselves when met with kindness or encouraged to talk and were listened to.

What Covid-19 taught us was a challenging but valuable lesson. Many of us collectively learnt insights that could stand us in good stead for future outbreaks of contagious disease, horrific wars or massive economic downturns. We learnt that the power of human connection, more than any other strategy, could help us deal with challenges beyond our control. We learnt that in the face of great personal hardship, we rarely hankered for 'stuff' or to acquire new things. We knew that what we were drawn towards to heal and salve our panicky minds and fearful hearts was contact with our people, our tribe.

Human connection is strengthened by our sharing our vulnerability and our truth. So, I urge you to reach out and share your truth with people you can trust to stand with you and be on your side.

How you can develop resilience

During therapy, I frequently introduce the idea of arenas, as already mentioned in this chapter. This is a simplified way of defining different aspects of the client's life. For instance, people can frequently understand what is meant by a work arena, including both the positive and negative aspects they experience in the workplace. Within the work arena they might also focus on their ambitions for their career and any stumbling blocks or issues that feel challenging.

A personal life arena could include family, friends and romantic interests. This arena most closely reflects your current life stage. Is your personal life arena occupied by the trials and tribulations of dating, or are you trying to balance your emotional needs while raising a young family or coming to terms with loss after a partner dies or your key relationship has broken down?

You can see that within these various arenas, your attention shifts and refocuses on whatever your current concerns are.

You might agree that the transparency of a healthy work arena, or your much-loved sports/hobby arena, feels more manageable and easier to navigate than the 'Wild West' of your personal life arena, where frequently there are no rules. In your personal life arena, you can be confronted by other people's unpredictable behaviour or lack of personal accountability. Compared to a work arena where you feel you are thriving and your achievements are recognised, your personal relationship arena can feel hard to navigate. It's easy to understand why many people focus more on their careers than on finding their life partner. This is especially true when someone has a poorly developed sense of resilience; building personal relationships or forming friendships can be triggering and distressing when met with casual thoughtlessness or a lack of care.

Dealing with these challenges can frequently lead to a person developing a pattern of self-sabotaging behaviour or negative limiting beliefs that hinder their ability to meet a significant other to whom they can commit. For instance, it might feel safer to hold back or not be authentic with a new love interest. It might be an unconscious strategy for keeping yourself emotionally secure but could also hamper you from deeply connecting with another person?

It is common for many people with an underdeveloped sense of self-worth to experience heightened anxiety, people-pleasing behaviour including avoiding confrontation, and the helpful catch-all, 'Adult failure to thrive', especially when meeting and getting to know people in their personal arena. Add into this a tendency to rely on alcohol or illegal drug use to boost confidence, and this makes for a potentially complex mix of maladaptive strategies to cope with or hide their vulnerability.

So, strengthening one's innate sense of resilience is crucial for emotional wellbeing. The great news is that, with the fantastic adaptability of humans, if you didn't learn to be resilient in your childhood you can learn the key attributes for being resilient now, as an adult. Life is easier with resilience at your core, and this book teaches you how to develop, perhaps for the first time, new ways of thinking and feeling about yourself. You need no longer feel buffeted by the vagaries of what life throws at you. You will feel equipped and believe you have traction and influence over your own life. The way to build resilience is detailed in the up-and-coming sections, starting with 'How to use this book' below, providing you with a pathway of easy-to-action steps to make the changes that will benefit you the most.

How to use this book

This book is a practical guide to developing the skills you need to increase your sense of resilience and ability to trust your instincts in the face of adversity. It also provides a deeper understanding of the environment and circumstances that resilience needs in which to be nurtured naturally in childhood. It offers powerful therapy tools and processes to help develop in adulthood a resourceful mental attitude, however poor and unfavourable your early years' experience may have been.

Setting yourself up to succeed

To give yourself the best chance of succeeding with the tasks in this book, it's important to prepare yourself for victory. Think of yourself as a dedicated Ninja warrior in training. To give yourself the best chance to change how you think and feel about yourself, consider first that working through this book will take between 10 and 12 weeks, with you dedicating a minimum of 30 minutes per week. During this time, prioritise your self-care strategies, such as regular exercise, healthy eating, enough sleep and reducing alcohol intake to support your overall wellbeing. All of this will help as you work through the challenges ahead.

Choosing the right time to start your self-help journey is crucial. If you're already feeling overwhelmed at work or emotionally drained at home, it's best to wait until you have more mental and emotional capacity. Working consistently through the book, even if it is for less than an hour a week, is key. Avoid trying to fit your self-help time into an already jam-packed schedule. Rushing through the exercises may lead you to discover emotions or insights you don't have time to fully process or integrate.

On the next page is a draft contract you could consider signing. It clearly outlines the self-care considerations that it would be helpful for you to adopt and it succinctly outlines the pledge you are making to yourself.

Once you're ready to begin, you can use the dedicated pages in this book to record your notes. Alternatively, buy yourself a notebook if you prefer to record your reflections and insights separately. Use your handwritten notes to record your feelings and also to give yourself credit for your a-ha moments and the progress you make. Taking the time to note down and celebrate your progress, no matter how small it may seem, demonstrates compassion for yourself, one of the keystones this book wants you to achieve.

You will need to find a private and comfortable space where you can dedicate uninterrupted time for at least 30 minutes a week to exploring your thoughts and feelings. While focusing on the exercises in the book, taking regular breaks is essential to process any emotions that come to the fore. Many people successfully resolve past trauma and transform their thinking and feelings about themselves by taking things in incremental stages. Be kind to yourself every step of the way. Remember, the results from therapeutic work are not always immediately apparent, and this is particularly true in self-guided work like this. Once you have committed to starting, you need to trust the process and give yourself the time and space to benefit fully from this period of exploration.

Commitment contract for increasing my resilience

I, ..., recognise that I am ready to prioritise my mental and emotional wellbeing. As I embark on this self-help journey using The Getting of Resilience, I acknowledge that real change requires commitment and consistency.

I hereby commit to setting aside at least 30 minutes each week for 10 weeks to work through *The Getting of Resilience* using the tools and exercises for self-reflection.

For my sessions, I will find a quiet, private space to tune into my inner experience without distraction or judgement.

I understand that some weeks, I may not feel like making time for self-care. However, I accept that transformation emerges from small, regular steps forward. By signing below, I affirm my dedication to caring for myself during this pivotal time of personal growth. I deserve to feel empowered from within.

I also recognise that this exploration can sometimes bring up challenging emotions. I commit to approaching this work with gentleness, patience and compassion towards myself. I cannot expect to change lifelong patterns overnight. If this programme is overwhelming, I will consider breaking the work into smaller steps or reducing the frequency. Should any exceptionally painful issues arise, I will also consider working with a therapist to heal past wounds with professional support. My wellbeing involves honouring my limits while regularly devoting time to positive change.

Signature ....

Date...............................

Order of work

The real work begins with gathering information and insights in Chapter 2: The impact of family on resilience. This is a chance to become a detective of your psychology by learning some common characteristics of dysfunctional families and seeing if any of the characteristics resonate with your own experience. You may want to read through parts of this chapter a couple of times and use the first Worksheet, 'Worksheet 1: Family stories' on page 24, or use its prompts to handwrite in your notebook your reflections on your family story and the story you tell yourself.

There is a second worksheet at the end of this section (page 32) called 'Worksheet 2: The impact of the family on resilience – having your needs met', that invites you to explore the theory of an important psychological construct called Maslow's Hierarchy of Needs for child development and to consider if your needs were adequately met as a child.

Chapter 3: The biology of resilience, explores how trauma and labelling young people can cause them to act out or to become submissive 'people-pleasers' as strategies for survival. Again, the book asks you to be information-gathering and open to insights and a-ha moments in this section. The Worksheet at the end of this chapter, 'Worksheet 3: The biology of resilience – memories and recollections', asks you to recall and note down what challenges you faced growing up. If you remember these events, memories or conclusions about yourself as an adult, then they were influential to you as a child, so they count.

In Chapter 4: The timeline protocol, you are introduced to a way of using some of your insights and recollections from Chapters 1 and 2 and to plot them along a simple timeline that can help give you clarity when you look back over your life. You will discover times in your life when you felt in balance and other times when you felt overwhelmed or even self-sabotaged in your relationships or your working life. You can discover from this process that events were not coincidental, but you might work out a pattern of behaviour that you've been repeating.

The Timeline is a rich seam to explore. The details of how to create your own Timeline are at the end of this chapter in Worksheet 4: Timeline protocol –

instructions (page 48). To access the powerful insights that result from this might require you dedicating several of your work sessions over a few weeks to doing this. In fact, the Timeline protocol benefits from being revisited. It is almost as if, once you allow yourself to explore your past milestones and any emotional load those events still carry for you, then other memories pop up too.

When you've reached this point in the book, you will have worked through three Chapters all designed with the aim of gathering information, experiencing a-ha moments and being a detective of your own psychology. Hopefully you will have several pages of notes at this point, many of which may include events, memories or conclusions about yourself that feel negative or uncomfortable. So, with that in mind, now would be the perfect time to turn to Chapter 8: Emotional Freedom Technique (EFT). All the therapy approaches included in this book and the additional resources available with the website links (see page 135) have been tested over many years in my one-to-one work with clients, training sessions and group work.

Although I rarely work exclusively with EFT, sometimes aka 'Tapping', I value this approach as a gateway modality to help shift clients from their analytical left-brain thinking into their more intuitive, emotionally-connected right-brain thinking. EFT itself is part of a wider group of therapy approaches called Meridian Energy Therapies, all of which are highly effective and valuable for use in therapy sessions and for self-help when dealing with uncomfortable emotions. By including EFT in this book, I encourage you to learn how to use it as a tool for life. If you become distressed or overwhelmed by any of the emotions you are trying to unpick in connection with events and memories, you'll be able to 'tap' as a way of helping you feel more grounded and calmer.

As well as using tapping to work through difficult emotions, EFT is also a powerful tool for discovering deeply buried emotions. This therapy approach is fully explained here (page 93), along with a picture guide to help you learn how to do EFT yourself in How to practise EFT or 'Tapping' on pages 94-95, and there is a worksheet at the end of this section called Worksheet 8: EFT primer, which can help you establish what issue you want to tap on and how to get the best results from this therapy approach.

Looping back to regular content order, now we come to Chapter 5: Improving your self-belief. Here, you have an opportunity to explore the role of your inner voice and its impact on your self-esteem. In Worksheet 5: Transforming your inner voice at the end of the chapter (page 56), you will learn how to interrupt those negative thoughts that have been influencing how you think and feel about yourself. And, remember, if you have already leapt to Chapter 8, you can use EFT as a powerful therapeutic technique to transform negative self-talk.

Chapter 6: Resolving unhelpful thinking styles gives you an opportunity for further detective work into your psychology, allowing you to explore which of the 10 unhelpful thinking styles described most resonate with you. Then use Worksheet 6: Changing your thinking style to change how you think about yourself, on page 72.

Chapter 7: How to implement change, provides an opportunity, with Worksheet 7: Strategy focus (page 90), to identify where you need to focus your attention to build your resilience by choosing from the included strategies the ones that resonate the most with you. The key is to take actionable steps, however small, in the right direction today.

Chapter 8: Emotional Freedom Technique (EFT) has then already been described above. If you haven't already dived into learning EFT, now is the time.

Chapter 9: Hypnotherapy, refers to three MP3 audio recordings you will be able to access following the instructions in the resource section at the rear of the book (page 135). You can rotate listening to these three recordings or keep to one for at least a week before swapping. Hypnosis is also called 'suggestion therapy' and works most effectively when repeated for at least 21 days to embed powerful suggestions. After this period, choosing a recording to listen to every other day would be beneficial. There is no worksheet for this section; you must let your subconscious mind do the work.

Chapter 10: The power of forgiving, then includes the powerful mantra of Ho'oponopono (see page 113) and gives easy-to-follow instructions on how to use this ancient Polynesian method of forgiveness to free yourself. Worksheet 9: The list of unforgiven people at the end of that chapter (page 116) is a place to compile a list of all those you are currently refusing to forgive.

Chapter 11: The power of fierce gratitude, is an introduction to gratitude work, but not the timid, namby-pamby gratitude work you may have already come across. The act of fierce gratitude lifts the work from platitude to being life-changing. At the end of Chapter 11, Worksheet 10: Fierce gratitude list (page 124), is where you start to compile your personalised list.

2. The impact of family on resilience

Your family background offers a quick insight into how you define yourself. When introduced to a new person, you might begin chatting with each other about your profession and job talk might be your dominant, mutual focus. However, suppose you want to build a human connection or intimacy with a new person? In that case, you're more likely to offer more significant insights into who you are than just what you do. The quickest way to achieve this is to pivot the conversation towards sharing stories about your family background. What you say or don't say about your family is an indicator of how far you have come in your own life, or it can act to highlight how loyal you still are to your roots. Even the absence of a family can be a significant part of one's personal story.

How we were raised plays a big part in our personal, emotional, intellectual and social development. It is within our family that we are first exposed to potent influences in our life. These are often the ones that become the defining aspects of how we behave and our emotions, dreams and fears. In essence, this is how our identity is formed – the parts of ourselves that we share most widely and the aspects of ourselves that only a few close friends or family know about.

Everyone is shaped and moulded by their experience of growing up in their particular family structure. Your behaviour is influenced by the strategies you developed to cope with your unique familial pressures and expectations. We all understand that difficult things happen while growing up, and sometimes terrible things happen. Caring or careless parenting does not ultimately protect us from negative experiences in the big wide world. What makes the difference is the story we tell ourselves about those harrowing, challenging events we all inevitably have to deal with. It is the judgements about ourselves that we make that stay with us, and that script is often laid down insidiously at the heart of the family when we are young, unformed and powerless. Within the powerful dynamic of the family, we pick up the subtle and sometimes not-so-subtle expressions of expectation about who we are supposed to be and our place in the world.

Every family is different. The conventional structure of a mother and a father and one or more children is rarer nowadays than in the 1950s when most children were raised in nuclear families. Today, there are increasing numbers of single-parent families, step or blended families, families with two unmarried partners who are of the opposite sex or the same sex, adoptive families and official or informal foster families, as well as families where children are raised by another relative or by their grandparents.[1,2] Altogether 51% of children born in 2022 in England and Wales were born to unmarried mothers; that is more than those born in a marriage or civil partnership for the first time since records began in 1845. This is a massive societal shift when in the previous century alone, 'illegitimacy' and unmarried parenthood were associated with stigma, shame and disadvantage.

What makes a dysfunctional family

It's not the family structure that determines whether it will be a dysfunctional family or not. Other characteristics commonly found in the dynamics of unhealthy families can be witnessed across the variety of family structures. It is also worth noting that if these dynamics are left unexplored, they can become embedded family behaviour patterns that pass from generation to generation. I often work with clients who, through their therapy work, dedicate themselves to understanding and discovering the often unspoken rules by which their unhappy and sometimes seriously dysfunctional families operate. They, through extraordinary personal courage, become the person who calls time on intergenerational harm. With the insight they have developed and their determination, they break the hold of the dysfunctional patterns they've grown up with so that future generations do not have to experience what they lived through. It takes guts to reject everything you've known and forge a new, uncharted path, but it can be done.

Key types of dysfunctional family behaviour

So, having already established that every family is different, dysfunctional families are oddly similar, albeit on a spectrum or sliding scale where those at either end of the scale are the most challenging. Many factors contribute to family dysfunction, including some of the major issues listed below that separate families and would influence every aspect of how they function.

- Physical or sexual abuse
- Alcoholism and drug abuse
- Chronic illness, including mental health challenges.

Common characteristics of a dysfunctional family include an inability to listen to each other or express authentic feelings with each other, which can leave children growing up feeling unheard and unvalued. Some families never speak of anything beyond the mundane, and others are quick to temper so that any conversations quickly escalate to being shouty and stressful. Exchanges where adults talk in a monologue that doesn't invite participation, can feel particularly crushing for children as they quickly learn their opinion or their views are not sought or acknowledged. Children learn to be quiet at a very early age, absolutely understanding on an unconscious level that they will not be able to share their inner world without being criticised or worse.

Other dysfunctional families communicate by proxy. They rarely, if ever, speak authentically with each other about what is really bothering them but will readily speak furiously or passionately about politics or football. It is similar to the war in Syria or Ukraine, where world super-powers play out their mutual loathing of each other by funding and arming other countries' militaries. These armies then fight for their national goals while world leaders use proxy conflict to mask their global aspirations. Within some families, arguing about politics or sport becomes the proxy arena of discussion, the proxy topic where anger, upset and other uncomfortable emotions can be expressed while minimising the chances of authentic dialogue, which might risk collateral damage to the family members.

Banter and put-downs

Constant criticism directed at a child can feel undermining and more distressing than parents often realise. It can be subtle or not-so-subtle, such as teasing about height or weight or how they look, or it can be harsher still with comments used to damage a child's self-worth. Some parents consider how they berate or criticise their children to be banter and harmless. However, it can lead to a poor self-image and hinder a child's ability to develop resilience. Children raised in households where criticism is the common currency will often feel disempowered. They may attempt to bully other children in school to feel validated. They will have internalised the feeling of influential adults metaphorically punching down on them, and some children will replicate this behaviour in the outside world.

Never 'good enough'

Some children are raised in families where their achievements are never acknowledged as good enough. Parents lament their average children and their average academic or average sporting achievements. Messaging can be subtle or blatant, but young children internalise that they are not good enough or are a disappointment to their parents, who expect more of them. The constant criticism denies children the opportunity to be recognised for their unique selves with their personal strengths and weaknesses.

Some parents who struggle to overcome disadvantage or poverty place their offspring under immense pressure to achieve academic success and prowess in high-status professions they favour. I've worked with many profoundly dissatisfied and unhappy accountants, lawyers, doctors, engineers and pharmacists in their thirties and forties who, although seemingly successful in their careers, had always wanted to be actors, artists or dancers. Still, their parents categorically refused to allow them to express their preferences and persuaded or coerced them into compliance.

Controlling parents

This leads me to the dysfunctional family dynamic of children who are overly controlled by their parents or carers to the point where the direction of their natural interests is ignored, denied or obliterated over time. Many young people raised in a controlling family are denied the opportunity to discover and formulate their direction. The expectations of their controlling parents mould them, and that takes precedence over what they may have wanted for themselves. Eventually, many grow into adults who lack the necessary motivation to change or improve the situation they find themselves in in their adult life. The way controlling parents can inhibit their offspring's sense of autonomy means that adults raised in this way struggle to fully know who they are or recognise what they want out of their lives.

Addressing dysfunctional family behaviour

Clients I see who were raised in this dysfunctional family dynamic are often plagued with self-doubt and haunted by who they 'should' be versus who they want to be. They often come to a point in their life when they want to stop experiencing the pressure to comply. It can feel like a massive crisis, including suicidal ideation, as their family dynamic has never encouraged them to trust their judgement or listen to their intuition. What often happens is that they can flounder in adulthood, and they can find it challenging to commit to any particular career path, partner or lifestyle choice as they are never sure whether their motivation is authentically their own or imposed externally by either other people or circumstances.

Some controlling parents have a specific goal for their offspring to achieve. It can feel like a child's life was predetermined almost from birth as parents want them to fulfil a generational expectation, such as having their child become an Olympic-grade gymnast, a virtuoso musician or the world's greatest whatever – just as they had once been. Some children raised with the weight of this kind of mono-focus praise their parents for making them who they are today and believe if they hadn't been hot-housed from an early age, they would never have achieved their success. However, for every successful adult whose meteoric rise began as a child prodigy, encouraged or pushed by a parent or an authority figure to practise, rehearse or learn by rote when they'd rather have been doing something else or simply playing, there is probably at least one rebellious, non-compliant offspring who would have achieved more if they'd been trusted to choose to step up when they were ready.

Using fear

Adults who want dominance and control over their children may do so through the threat of, or with, violence. They may also respond unpredictably so that a child is never sure how their parents will react to them. This shape-shifting chaos leaves children fearful and watchful as they attempt to 'read' the adults. When power within a family is fear-based, it can only lead to an emotionally unstable household, with children holding their collective breath before the next dreaded put down, shaming or physical hurt.

Divide and rule

As I said earlier, family dysfunction is on a spectrum. Scapegoating and making one child the butt of unfavourable comparisons while praising their siblings is divisive and deeply undermines a child's development of self-worth. It is only the worst cases of family favouritism that make the national news, when parents care for some of their offspring whilst leaving a sibling or other children severely neglected or uncared for. More commonly, a child is labelled by their parents or carers as the 'clumsy one', the 'slow learner', the 'troublesome child', or even 'the black sheep' of the family. I've seen many clients who struggled as adults with the confusion and hurt they felt about the unfairness they felt when their siblings were treated more favourably. Childhood rifts originate in either apparent or covert differences in treatment, and the feelings of injustice run deep and can often endure for decades.

Some families fuel misunderstanding by seemingly having greater or lesser ambitions for siblings. I've seen clients sent far away to boarding school while their brothers and sisters were schooled locally. Parents may have felt they were supporting a child who showed academic promise, but the boarded child felt isolated and believed they had been excluded from their family's day-to-day life through some fault of their own. The counterpart to this is when it is decided that a sibling should be educated locally instead of being sent to boarding school. Without knowing why their parents took this decision, it is unfortunately all too easy for the young person to tell themselves that their local schooling has been chosen because they lack academic ability. This young person's negative story about themselves will then be that they are without value and not worth investing time and money in to be educated in the same way as their siblings.

Time and time again, within family dynamics, we can see it's not the event or decision that can cause emotional harm but the lack of explanation or discussion that can lead a child to believe that they are at fault for the decision their elders have made on their behalf.

In my own life, as I describe in the Introduction, I was the victim of sexual abuse at the age of seven. Although my mother was almost immediately aware of what had happened, she did not talk to me then, and I did not find out for decades what steps she had taken to protect me. For all those years, I was ashamed and blamed myself for what had happened until, at last, I could discuss it with her and let go of all the limiting beliefs and self-doubt that had built up over the years. I, therefore, lived alone with trauma, an experience which had a seminal impact on my perception of myself as I grew up.

Worksheet 1: Family stories

Use this worksheet or your notebook to handwrite your reflections on your own family story and the stories you are prompted to tell yourself.

Key points to consider are:

- Do you make negative judgements about yourself from what happened in your family?
- Consider how your experience of growing up in your family shaped your identity.
- Recognise the coping strategies you may have developed due to how you were raised.

Case study 1: Sibling bullying and abuse

A client from Southern Spain suffered extreme trauma and post-traumatic stress disorder (PTSD) from living in a household where her elder brother terrorised her and her mother. His violent, unpredictable outbursts meant both women lived in fear as they constantly attempted to second-guess his mood and do whatever they needed to do to keep the peace. The daughter, my client, felt put at risk and undervalued by her mother, who she felt prioritised her brother over concerns for their safety. She regularly contacted external social service agencies, hoping they would intervene with her brother. At the same time, her mother made excuses for her son for years, playing down the domestic violence they suffered.

One day, long after my client had left home, her brother seriously attacked his by-now elderly mother and caused injuries that prompted the authorities to act. Even though he was removed from the house and offered a place in a hostel, his mother soon invited him back into the family home. The dynamic continued to be coercive and threatening, and my client stayed in touch with her mother by telephone and email but no longer visited as she didn't feel safe around her sibling.

This client benefited from learning that she could impose her own boundaries to protect herself. Although her decision to relocate to London and permanently leave Spain was painful, she also saw that sometimes withdrawing or limiting contact with her dysfunctional family was a powerful way to prioritise her needs. She recognised that prioritising her safety was something her mother had never been able to do for either herself or her. She was sad that she needed to disconnect physically from her mother but realised that she needed to take responsibility for her own safety.

Case study 2: Ruling with anger

Another family dynamic where one sibling's needs took priority over another's was with a young client of mine who had a slightly older sister diagnosed with autism. The older sister experienced erratic mood swings and had been violent, especially targeting my client, who had learnt to be afraid of her sister's potential to hurt her. Without speaking or formally deciding between themselves, the family and the household routines developed to help avoid or minimise the risk of the older sister losing her temper. With this dynamic in mind, home life followed a strict pattern as much as possible. It meant that meal times, including the types of food cooked and served and the seating positions at the table, were all determined by what her older sister demanded. If my client wanted to speak about her day at school with her mum during supper, her older sister's mood would quickly become agitated with the threat of almost immediate escalation of intimidating behaviour.

My client learnt to put her sister's needs above her own. She told herself that her mother wasn't interested in what she had to say. With the judgement she made, she chose to be mute when she came home from school. Over many months, she became more withdrawn, barely answering in more than one or two words when asked a direct question. Although she hid her emotions, she was increasingly anxious and depressed. She had also begun restricting her eating, and she said in an early therapy session that she felt increasingly alone and invisible.

My client felt guilty and ashamed that she longed to have time alone with her mum. Her mother's response to her made her feel unimportant and certainly not as important as the needs of her older sibling. It made my client feel there was little or no available time or interest in what she needed. She also decided she had no choice but to be the dutiful daughter, the quiet, well-behaved one, even though she felt desperately unhappy and emotionally abandoned by her family.

Sharing their truth

When I met this family, they were at a crisis point, with the younger daughter's burgeoning eating disorder becoming more entrenched. Her mother counteracted the story her daughter had told herself that she didn't count and reassured her that her needs were paramount.

The daughter's time in therapy encouraged her to speak her truth within a framework that meant her mother and father could listen. The parents could talk openly about how they had chosen to manage their elder daughter's challenging behaviour. They came up with and implemented a solution as to how their younger daughter could have time alone with either parent without her sister being present. This practical solution underpinned the adults' more comprehensive understanding and recognition of how challenging the dynamic had been at home. It led to them developing other strategies that worked better for their children.

This example shows how family circumstances, even though very challenging, were not as damaging to how my young client thought and felt about herself as was the assumption she had made that her mum didn't care about her. The practical adjustments her parents made to accommodate her emotional needs were initial steps to enable her to feel validated and loved. Once she had debunked the story she had told herself, my client could see how loved she was, which positively affected her self-esteem and sense of self-worth.

Conclusion

Power struggles such as those I've outlined here create dysfunction and unhappiness within a family. Children and young people who feel they are not valued by their adult carers or parents may commonly experience self-esteem issues, symptoms of depression or anxiety, and difficulty in regulating their emotions.

Reducing chaos

Children thrive when the environment meets their needs. Newborns are helpless at birth and are highly dependent on the adults in their life for every aspect of their care so that they can grow and eventually fulfil their potential as adults. An easy way to understand the myriad of needs required to flourish from childhood to adulthood was developed in the 1930s by American psychologist, Abraham Maslow. He created five loosely progressive categories, known as Maslow's Hierarchy of Needs.[3] These categories are illustrated like a pyramid, with the bottom layer called '1. Physiological needs'. This base layer includes all the practical aspects of life, such as shelter, food and clothing. A child cannot survive without their basic survival needs being met.

The next layer up as we climb the pyramid is '2. Safety needs'. This layer recognises that once physiological needs are met, the priority is to feel safe and secure within our environment. In real terms, this is about a child's emotional environment. Ideal circumstances would be where adult carers provide a safe environment because the adults emotional needs are also met.

Next up is '3. Sense of belonging'. This layer focuses on the abstract idea of belonging and feeling loved. The child in ideal circumstances is emotionally attached to their carer or carers who can equally meet the emotional needs of their young charges.

With the three foundational levels met, not even to the most favourable degree, the next layer comes into play. This is '4. Esteem needs', which means achieving recognition of abilities, respect from peers and appreciation of who we are in the broader world.

Finally, at the apex of the pyramid, is the highest level of potential human achievement. '5. Self-actualisation' means finding our authentic self and living our truth to the very best of our ability.

With reference to Maslow's Hierarchy of Needs, daily routines are more than just an efficient way of getting practical things done. A set bedtime, for instance, with a book, bath and bottle of milk for a young child, or a morning routine of washing, clothes to suit the season and breakfast, provide evidence that many of a child's basic survival needs are being met.

When a child is raised in a calm household where the parents or carers are emotionally stable and thriving themselves, then there is every possibility that a child's need for safety and security, as in level 2 above, is being met.

Parents or carers who interact with their young child to smile and give frequent verbal reinforcement and physical care fulfil the requirements outlined by Maslow in level 3 to engender a healthy sense of belonging.

Cumulatively, all the layers of Maslow's Hierarchy of Needs make up a child's requirements to grow into adulthood. With levels 1, 2 and 3 met, children feel secure, loved and valued, empowering them to venture forth from the heart of the family to confidently enjoy nursery or school, ready to learn and explore. These children also innately know that when it is time to return home, they will be cared for and loved as they are every day.

Fulfilling level 4 ensures a child can develop healthy self-esteem. Parents or primary carers can help realise this by encouraging belief in their child's abilities to complete tasks and achieve their goals in the wider world.

What Maslow called his level 5 – Self-actualisation – at the pyramid's apex, represents living our passion or commitment to fulfil our heart's desire.

Good enough parenting

The term 'good enough' parenting describes a concept that derives from the work of eminent English paediatrician and psychoanalyst Donald Winnicott.[4] Through his research on mothers and babies in the 1950s, Winnicott concluded that parents should gradually become less accommodating of their children's demands as they grow older and more independent. According to his findings, meeting a child's needs just 30% of the time is enough to raise happy, resilient children who feel securely attached. Essentially, Winnicott's theory states that taking care of a child's needs some of the time, but not constantly catering to them, helps children become more self-reliant and emotionally sturdy. A 'good enough' level of responsiveness, not perfection, allows children to flourish.

Winnicott's findings align with Maslow's Hierarchy of Needs and how none of the needs illustrated in the pyramid need to be achieved 100% for a child to thrive. For all sorts of reasons, performing elements in any of the layers in Maslow's pyramid, even to a barely optimal degree or varying levels of achievement, children can go on to be resilient and achieve their potential. So, how is that?

Maslow's creation is just one way of explaining a complex process. In my work with clients, for those who were raised in a household where some of the elements within levels 1, 2 and 3 were not consistently met or were unreliable, some young people experienced encouragement to believe in themselves from a grandparent, teacher, sports coach or music tutor that proved to be adequate to overcome many material and emotional disadvantages in their home life.

Worksheet 2:
Having your needs met

Use the worksheet or your notebook to handwrite your thoughts on how well your needs were met in your family.

Key points to consider are:

- Were routines present in your family to create a feeling of security?
- Reflect on your experience of feeling loved or not while growing up.
- Identify ways your self-esteem was supported or undermined in your family structure.

3. The biology of resilience

It isn't only trauma, deprivation or abuse that impacts one's ability to develop inner resilience. Society accepts that life-threatening events such as a car accident, natural disaster or act of violence can change people emotionally forever. However, emotional or psychological trauma is often not caused by a single, isolated incident. It can be much less dramatic and more mundane events that leave a lasting effect.

Changes to the brain's ability to bounce back from adversity are commonly the result of cumulative negative interactions during childhood, which can leave young people vulnerable to mental illness. The world-famous trauma theorist Bessel van der Kolk explains these negative interactions during childhood by describing how prolonged or repeated trauma disrupts the brain's normal development and growth processes and impairs its ability to synthesise sensory input, emotions and thoughts into an integrated understanding.

De Kolk acknowledges that trauma has the most impact during what is understood to be the most highly sensitive years of a child's development. During this period, essential regulatory functions are developed, and brain structures, neural pathways and connections are formed, or, in effect, 'turned off'. This critical age range has been identified as being from birth to three years of age.

Although the brain does retain 'plasticity', or the ability to change and adapt, well into adulthood, this is a life-defining period of influence which makes interventions for long-term improvements more challenging. During this time, an infant learns how to regulate and recognise their own emotions and those of others. The quality of nurturing that children experience during these crucial years can also influence their ability to handle stress.

Human nature drives survival

Human nature drives an infant towards a desire for attachment to their mother or primary carer. This desire is forgiving enough that the infant will adapt to the parenting style they experience as it is all they know. When we consider how much can go astray in the dynamics of the child/adult relationship within a healthy family dynamic, the possibilities for emotional damage to an infant are vast. However, we are socialised through our experiences of these primary relationships.

An infant will process the abuse or neglect they experience as if it's their fault and conclude there must be something innately wrong, bad or shameful about them. If the nurturing is absent or compromised through some of the parental circumstances detailed earlier, the infant will assume they are at fault and not their carers. Again, it is worth a reminder that when we think of abuse, it is easy to jump to the extremes of sexual or violent abuse committed against infants and children. However, the casual cruelties perpetrated by a thoughtless or overwhelmed or emotionally absent parent or primary caregiver, such as withdrawal of love from a child, can lead to complex trauma responses. The more aware children are, the more likely they are to try to make sense of their experiences by internalising feelings of shame and blaming themselves.

Bessel van der Kolk's research has led him and his researchers to believe that trauma stays within the body and influences a person's view of the world. It is as if the trauma lies beneath conscious awareness and can be triggered again in adulthood in situations similar to those in which the original trauma occurred. For instance, losing a friendship or the unwanted breakup of a romantic relationship can cause a tsunami of intense feelings of shame or rejection that far exceed those the current situation warrants.

An enduring effect of trauma in childhood is being continuously on the lookout for signs you may be in danger. You are, in effect, hyper-vigilant, and this is caused by the autonomic nervous system activated in infancy from feelings of not being safe. In this state, your body is flooded with a biochemical response that includes hormones such as adrenalin and cortisol, making you feel agitated and anxious. Children and young adults who have experienced developmental trauma can be triggered into states of high anxiety by events or even interpretations of events that another person who benefited from a non-traumatic childhood might not even register.

Sometimes trauma is passed on unintentionally from the parent to the child, so they are both vulnerable and can be readily triggered to experience distressing emotions. This emotional pain is known as intergenerational trauma. If a parent has experienced harsh parenting and has not resolved their chronic feelings of shame and self-blame, they may pass the same negative feelings on to their children. This kind of behaviour happens below the level of conscious awareness as the parent or carer has normalised their behaviour or isn't aware that they are constantly triggered to have negative feelings.

Passing on pain to new generations

Parents with unresolved trauma often find themselves confronted by strong unintegrated emotions that throw them into a state of overwhelm where they feel out of control. As well as placing them under tremendous pressure, it negatively impacts their children. Kolk explains: 'Babies are particularly attuned to their primary carer and will sense their fear and traumatic stress; this is particularly the case where violence is present in the family. The baby will be unsettled and therefore more demanding of an already overwhelmed parent.' The parent's negative emotions are frequently expressed non-verbally through facial expressions, the tenor of their voice and touch, all of which are influenced by their underlying emotional state.

I am not talking here about the circumstances of one day, a sharp word, or a careless gesture. What potentially damages a child's self-esteem is an accumulation of hostile gestures and non-verbal signals originating in their parent or primary carer's unresolved trauma. Van der Kolk clearly makes his point when he explains that, when children endure stressful situations for extended periods of time, it can result in 'toxic stress' that negatively impacts their brain development. Specifically, it makes children more reactive to future stressful events, increases their activity levels and hinders their capacity for learning, focusing and relating to other people in a trusting way. The prolonged exposure fundamentally impairs children's ability to form healthy attachments and relationships.

How children react to trauma

In young people, childhood trauma can show up as self-destructive behaviour. They can be disruptive, non-compliant and challenging. School can be a demanding environment for children who have experienced trauma. They can often be at odds with the institution's rules from early on. Their difficulty concentrating or sitting still and behaving appropriately in class will mark them for criticism. They may also have trouble developing and maintaining friendships, and they can be vulnerable to bullying by either becoming a target for bullies or becoming bullies themselves.

Van de Kolk describes how young people who have suffered childhood trauma are frequently disadvantaged in mainstream educational settings. He explains that children who experience trauma often struggle to manage their actions and emotions. Their distress makes it challenging for them to self-regulate in order to relax or comfort themselves. As a result, these children are frequently seen as overly active or hyperactive. The root cause is their traumatic experiences rather than an inherent tendency towards excessive energy and movement.

Other unhelpful labels applied to traumatised young people are that they are oppositional, rebellious, unmotivated and anti-social. These challenging behaviours are strategies the traumatised young person has developed to minimise their emotional distress. How adults in authority respond and manage these young people's behaviour can cause them to be labelled 'problem children' and lead to further stigmatisation and trauma. Some young people with a background of early developmental trauma can turn to drugs and alcohol to numb the overwhelming negative feelings they experience about themselves. By self-medicating with drugs and alcohol, they are perpetually clouding their sense of awareness and effectively dampening the expression of their authentic feelings. Unsurprisingly this creates more problems than it solves.

Young people can be further stigmatised and cast out if they show aggressive or antisocial behaviour. Challenging behaviour can become a tragic downward spiral for some young people as their behaviour worsens, and the consequences potentially grow more serious. Even though they are very vulnerable, they can be challenging, angry and destructive. They can be a danger to themselves and others. Without early intervention, they can face tragic circumstances. They can feel lost to us, to broader society, and, of course, to themselves. As society's response to their behaviour becomes more punitive, it is easy for young people with this kind of negative childhood experience to convince themselves that they deserve the treatment meted out to them because, subconsciously, they believe they are worthless and intrinsically wrong.

Conversely, not all young people with childhood trauma act out. Some are compliant and show people-pleasing behaviour. They are vulnerable in a different way. They may suffer anxiety and depression later in life. They may self-harm or suffer from an eating disorder. Their inner trauma is like a guarded secret they are very good at keeping to themselves. They can be perfectionists who equate their self-worth with academic achievement or judge themselves as worthy by the number on their bathroom scales. Using external validation does not overcome their feelings of imposter syndrome.

These young people are plagued by self-doubt despite excelling academically and achieving career promotions. They never believe they are good enough and often feel that one day everyone will discover they are a fraud. They are also vulnerable to stress and have difficulty managing change. They may well decide on a career that they think will give them recognition in society, such as medicine or law, where their role of caring for or assisting others less fortunate than themselves can feed their impoverished sense of self-worth. However, all their success rings hollow, as no professional acclaim will ever silence the inner voice that constantly reminds them how worthless they are.

How childhood trauma and impaired emotional development manifest later in life is complex, and the behaviour of these young people can be bewildering and distressing to those who care about them. Often it is easier to focus on the behaviour, such as drug use or self-harm or anorexia, than it is to focus on the underlying issues. However, the underlying problems drive their maladaptive behaviour. Resolving their trauma is critical to enable building resilience from the inside out.

Growing up

You inevitably bring your childhood's negative and positive experiences with you as you go into adulthood. Negative experiences can be particularly influential when people commonly choose life partners who remind them of, or feel familiar with, their family dynamics. Referring to judgements formulated about yourself when growing up can expose you to unhelpful triggers later in life. For instance, a child who experienced criticism and unrealistic expectations growing up can feel disproportionally triggered as an adult when criticised by their partner.

The irony is that much of the family dynamic you struggled with throughout your childhood can be played out in the opinions and criticisms of the family you have created for yourself in adulthood. Suppose your emotional response to criticism or negative judgements often feels excessive in the opinion of those who love you and whose opinion you trust. In that case, you are likely being triggered by old memories and feelings. The clue to whether or not this applies to you is how you manage conflict in your intimate relationships.

In the workplace, written and implied rules of conduct dictate how colleagues behave and communicate with each other. Within the work arena, emotional responses are muted or disguised to whatever degree is necessary to comply with your particular work culture. This is why your emotional reactions are usually masked when you feel unsupported, undermined, bullied or unfairly treated as an employee in a toxic work culture. Emotional detachment or passive-aggressive behaviour is the most common emotional response to a bullying boss or unsupportive colleagues. It is more usual to internalise emotional reactions in the workplace to survive negative experiences whilst holding on to your job. Unexpressed internalised emotions, however, tend to manifest as depression and anxiety.

In the arena that represents your personal life, there are no universally accepted rules of engagement. In fact, there are barely any rules at all. Each and every one of us has to develop our own code of conduct and sense of morality. It is up to you to decide how you want to behave towards others and also what behaviour is acceptable to those you choose to share your life with. With your closest emotional relationships, triggers from old painful memories are the most conspicuous. The old saying, 'memories buried alive never die', is never more accurate than with painful memories from childhood.

An example is if you descend rapidly into the 'red mist of anger'. If you are unsure how it is your anger becomes so out of control or you feel unable to interrupt the trajectory of your fury, you are likely experiencing triggers from your past. Another clue that your response is not proportionate to the current event is if you are able to notice how shocked and emotionally distressed your loved ones are by the extent of your outbursts. If this is the case, then it is likely your current emotions are being triggered by old memories or events, and because of this, your responses are intensified.

Unresolved emotional triggers can seriously impact the quality and sustainability of your current relationships. If you recognise these tendencies in yourself, rest assured you can resolve and release these old flashpoints so that you can be free to respond authentically and appropriately in the present without the additional emotional load from the past.

It's essential to be a detective of your own psychology and be curious about how your past experiences may influence you in the present. A very effective way of doing this is the NLP (Neuro-linguistic Programming) technique called the 'timeline protocol'. This protocol, discussed in detail in the next chapter, can be used to address many different issues. I've used it successfully with clients to track when they felt more balanced with their eating, for instance, and when they struggled with bingeing. I've also used this approach for clients to gain insights into their feelings of anxiety or depression. I recommend it as a way to explore whatever challenges you face with uncomfortable emotions.

Worksheet 3: Memories and recollections

Use the worksheet or your notebook to handwrite your recollections, memories or conclusions you have made about yourself growing up.

Key points to consider are:

- Consider how even seemingly small negative interactions in childhood impact you now.
- Recognise your early childhood sensitivity or who you were as a child.
- Recall how you behaved and what your behaviour was trying to say to your parents or carers.

4. The timeline protocol

The timeline protocol is a method of exploring when in your life you have felt in balance and when you have felt challenged by events, memories or conclusions about yourself. It will allow you to recall if you were triggered at the time of those events to behave in ways that were unhelpful to yourself or even self-sabotaging. It can also highlight any negative judgements or conclusions you made about yourself concerning those events or memories that affect you in the present.

Case study 3: A childhood trauma triggered in adulthood

The emotional trauma of an unpredictable family dynamic might lie dormant in a person's subconscious mind for a long time until something often entirely unconnected acts as a trigger.

A Danish client came to me with severe anxiety affecting her ability to work as a freelance photographer. When I saw her, she was in her mid-30s. She was an established, successful photojournalist who had travelled independently for years. She had never experienced these debilitating symptoms before. They affected most aspects of her life and included insomnia, catastrophic thinking and debilitating panic attacks that left her vulnerable and insecure. She had no idea what event had caused her to experience these uncomfortable feelings.

I began my therapy approach by using the timeline protocol. We started by drawing a straight line on a blank piece of paper, as I have included in the instructions on page 48. We started with her date of birth at the left-hand end of the line, and the right-hand represented the present. I enquired about critical events during her life, prompting her to consider if anything that had happened to her in the past had felt familiar to how she was currently feeling. We used the milestones she recalled, such as starting school; moving house; leaving home; getting married; deaths of close relatives etc, to focus on remembering how she had felt at those critical times. I encouraged her to be a detective of her psychology and to see if there were any links she could discover.

Plotting a life

The timeline format helped her very quickly identify the first time she had had a panic attack, about a year earlier. She was able to recall the memory in great detail. She said she had been commissioned to photograph a world-famous cave system in China known for its impressive stalactites and stalagmites. As the cave's experienced guides accompanied her, she felt increasingly unnerved at the head of each wooden staircase she was required to navigate. She found herself pausing at the head of the stairs and breathing deeply before she could continue to descend. The steps were well-lit and expertly constructed with a strong rope affixed to the cave's wall that made her descent as safe as possible, yet she had felt increasingly uneasy. She described the growing dread and queasy feeling in the pit of her stomach. I gently enquired if the feelings she had experienced at the top of the underground staircases felt familiar. Immediately her expression changed, and she said it reminded her of the stairs in the house she grew up in as a child living with her mother and father.

As a young girl, my client had made herself wake earlier than her mother to go downstairs before her and clean up the worst excesses of her father's drinking before her mother found out. Every day she remembered she used to stand at the top of the stairs and listen to the aggressive arguments between her mother and father. Her father was an alcoholic, and her mother would shout and remonstrate with him when she found him collapsed on the floor amid the chaos of his drinking. Although committed to protecting her father, she felt dread and fear about going downstairs as she never knew what she would find. Often he'd be covered in vomit and occasionally blood or worse. The stressful present-day experience of the staircases in the cave system had triggered her old feelings of fear and dread from her chaotic childhood.

I then focused our therapy work on resolving and releasing the trauma she had felt as a young girl dealing with her father's alcoholism; after that she was free of any further panic attacks or feelings of dread. Working with her was an excellent example of 'memories buried alive, never die'.

Timeline tips

When working on your timeline, dates are not necessary. Instead, focus on your life's critical milestones and then put them in the most accurate chronological order. Take the time needed to recall how you felt when those events unfolded, and consider acknowledging any enduring impact on how you think and feel about yourself today.

Here are some milestones from previous clients' work that could be relevant to your timeline. I've listed a sample of events that commonly create negative self-judgements or can also initiate negative behaviours.

- Breakdown of your parents' relationship
- Experiences of death and loss
- Uncomfortable or confusing sexual attention
- Traumatic experiences or events, either experienced first-hand or witnessed
- Bullying at school or in the workplace
- Puberty and physical changes
- Serious accidents or periods of illness
- Leaving home
- Feeling out of your depth and overwhelmed
- Financial stress
- Birth of your own children
- Relationship breakdown
- Redundancy.

Life events are legion on a continuum from birth to the present day. You will have your unique history, and I invite you to consider your critical events alongside how you think and feel about yourself now. Unresolved emotional pain from your past will be conspicuous from the depth of your emotional responses as you do this work. You may also identify patterns that you rely on in times of great personal stress to distract yourself. These maladaptations include increased alcohol or drug use, or excessive shopping, gambling or hoarding. A clue to help you know what to include are events of which you have vivid memories or recollections that you can still recall in detail. In your role as detective of your own psychology, the insights offered by undertaking the timeline protocol can be the beginning of realising the source of old and entrenched behaviour patterns that no longer serve you.

Worksheet 4: Timeline protocol – Instructions

Draw a straight line across the centre of this page, or use a blank piece of paper. Turn the page to horizontal format so you can draw a longer line. The lefthand end of the line represents your birth, and the righthand end represents today. (You may of course need more than one sheet of paper.)

From the work you have already done in Chapters 2 and 3, you will have refreshed your memory about your early years and other important life events. Now it is time to chronologically plot each one that feels significant on the timeline.

Although you probably have few or even no memories of yourself as a baby or very young child, think about what family legends or stories surrounded your birth and early years. Do you remember hearing if you were a hale and hearty baby? Or were you premature or unwell? Were you adopted as a young child? Who raised you, and was your care fractured or consistent?

Key points to consider are:

- As you select the milestones in your life and add them to your timeline, pause long enough to gain awareness of each event. Did this event make you feel emotionally in balance or remind you of feeling overwhelmed and out of control?
- As well as milestones, be aware of any patterns of behaviour you notice. For instance, have you had periods of time when you distracted yourself by being hyper-busy? Or when you drank too much alcohol? Took part in sexual behaviour that put you at risk? Took Class A drugs? Avoided opportunities? Suffered poor sleep? Procrastinated? There are many ways you can sabotage yourself and stop or hinder yourself from achieving your goals.

Once you have completed your timeline, spend as much time as you need to discover if any milestones or memories still hold an emotional charge for you. If they do then score them from zero to 10, with zero meaning no emotional discomfort and 10 being the most uncomfortable.

And, by the way, this is not an opportunity to beat yourself up about past unhelpful behaviours. We all only ever do the best we can do. Even when our best is not very good, it is all we have. Some things we've done or still do have been survival responses in times of great stress. This exercise is to shine a light, to breathe deeply and see what events, memories or conclusions might impact your ability to achieve self-fulfilment and happiness today.

The work you have achieved with your timeline can provide valuable insights into your emotional landscape. It exposes memories buried alive that still feel raw and cause you emotional pain in the present, even though they could have happened many decades earlier.

Create a separate list, on paper, of all the events, milestones or conclusions you've made about yourself on your timeline. Evaluate each aspect to determine if any uncomfortable emotions remain using a SUD (subjective unit of discomfort) rating of zero to 10, with zero indicating no discomfort and 10 indicating the worst negative feeling possible.

In Order of Work on page 12, it is recommended at this point in the book that you turn to Chapter 8: Emotional Freedom Technique (page 93) and learn this powerful therapy approach to help you release and resolve negative emotions associated with painful and uncomfortable memories. The aim is to utilise this self-help technique to prevent being triggered again by past events, allowing you to genuinely and suitably respond to current situations without being adversely affected by previous experiences. As a suggestion, initially focus on events from your timeline that rank low to medium on the SUD score as you familiarise yourself with the EFT technique. As you gain confidence and experience success with EFT, you can advance to addressing and releasing events, memories and conclusions that currently hold higher levels of emotional distress. The ultimate goal is to achieve a point where past events no longer have any power over you; though the memories may remain, they no longer hold any emotional turbulence.

5. Improving your self-belief

The idea of 'self-belief' is a popular aspiration for many people today, along with achieving Zen-like mindfulness or lithely moving from downward-facing dog to sun-salutation without as much as breaking into a sweat. All these goals sound great in theory, and why wouldn't anyone want to believe in themselves?

People frequently assume that self-belief is effortless for everyone to achieve, and if that were true, then everyone would just be getting on with it, and it wouldn't be a thing. But it is a thing. Self-belief doesn't feel like a natural state for many people, and perhaps struggling to achieve it can feel like just another way of beating yourself up for failing at something you think everyone else is managing to do as if they were born to it! Rest assured, many people struggle with achieving self-belief, just as they find yoga sweaty and uncomfortable.

The role of your inner voice

Low self-esteem, often caused by a critical and judgemental inner voice, goes hand in hand with self-doubt and imposter syndrome. The first thing that usually happens when I mention an inner voice to a client is that they look at me quizzically, and I can almost hear them saying to themselves, 'Well, I don't have an inner voice'. And that is their inner voice. Our unique inner voice developed during childhood. Each of us has a unique inner voice that speaks to us inside our minds, providing us with a running commentary on everything we say and do. We have become so accustomed to it chatting away in our mind that what it mostly says happens below our conscious awareness, and we barely pay it any notice.

That is fine if you have an inner voice that says, 'Oh, it doesn't matter that I didn't get that promotion I went for', or 'Oh shucks, I just pranged the car bumper on that post', and then goes on to say, 'Oh well, I'm still a fabulous person', or 'Amazing, my reactions were so fast I've only caused minimal damage to my car!'

From those examples of what an encouraging inner voice might say, I can tell you two things straight away:

1. Your mental health is in pretty good shape to have an inner voice that doubles as your biggest cheerleader, and
2. Most likely, you are not one of my clients.

The clients I work with have an inner voice that is much more carping and self-critical and is like a leaking tap dripping toxicity into their minds at every opportunity.

Listening to yourself

How do you find out what kind of inner voice you have? Firstly, assessing how negative versus positive your inner voice is, is helpful. In my therapy room, I have a simple visual aid for this. I have a large glass round fishbowl half-filled with gold and blue marbles on my desk. The fishbowl represents your mind, and the marbles represent your kind and unkind thoughts about yourself.

Psychologists estimate that a person's self-esteem is linked to their thoughts and feelings about themselves in the previous two weeks. So I'd like to ask you to imagine I sent you a large, round glass fishbowl a couple of weeks ago. I want you to imagine starting with an empty fishbowl, and every time you have a life-affirming, generous or kind thought about yourself, you drop in a gold marble, and every time you have a negative, self-deprecating or unkind thought about yourself, you drop in a blue marble. I want you to imagine that we have the fishbowl today, two weeks later. Studying it, I want you to imagine a mix of 100 gold and blue marbles inside. Now I want you to take an intuitive guess off the top of your head to ascertain what percentage of the marbles are gold versus what percentage are blue.

So, what would your percentage mix of blue and gold marbles be? If the percentages are similar to 70% blue versus 30% gold or 80% blue versus 20% gold, or even 98% blue versus 2% gold, as clients have told me, you too will be prone to imposter syndrome and not feeling that you are good enough. Anything more than a low percentage of blue marbles indicates your inner voice or self-talk is pretty hard on you, and the more blue marbles you have, the harsher your inner voice is. A judgemental and carping inner voice can be the source of so much of your self-doubt and imposter-syndrome anxiety.

Fortunately, you can erase your negative inner voice and replace it with an influential inner cheerleader that encourages you in your life rather than putting you down and making you feel like an imposter all of the time.

How to erase your negative inner voice

Assessing your percentage of positive self-talk versus negative self-talk is essential to transforming your inner voice. I recommend that you make a note on your smartphone or in a notebook of every negative thought you have about yourself for five days. Taking your time to consider your inner voice means that every time you say something self-deprecating or harsh about yourself during those five days, you no longer let that thought have free rein in your subconscious mind without making a conscious note of what your inner voice is saying to you.

As you note those negative, carping and judgemental thoughts, I encourage you to look for patterns or threads that tie them together and be open to noticing where the critical voice originates. If you are still unsure where the negative voice originated, you can use your notes to explore your psychology and examine your negative inner voice's language. Does it use slang words? Does it speak in a particular accent?

Who does your inner voice remind you of?

The inner voice has had free rein in your subconscious mind for years, possibly decades. Once you know the origin of your inner negative voice, it's time to interrupt it. The source of your inner voice is often a parent, grandparent or teacher; it's not even your voice! As I've already explained, negative self-talk happens below your conscious awareness. That drip of toxic put-downs and unkindness can be at the core of imposter syndrome and self-doubt. It's almost impossible for you to trust your capabilities and feel resilient when your self-talk is harsh and critical of you. It's often old, cruddy stuff from long ago that says more about the person you identified as the originator of your inner voice than it can ever say about you. So, the next time a negative, self-destructive thought comes into your mind, I encourage you to interrupt it and not allow it free rein in your subconscious mind anymore. To do this, you need to pay attention to what you think so that you can spot anything negative your inner voice says and contest it because it's not the truth.

When a negative thought comes to mind, I encourage you to acknowledge the thought you have had. Then, and this is most important, admit to yourself that it's not true and actively dismiss it from your thinking. To effectively dismiss a negative thought, I suggest you make a noise when you notice negative self-talk. You can make a game show buzzer noise, like when an answer is wrong. Actively rejecting the thought sends a solid message to your subconscious to dismiss that rubbish thought.

It doesn't take long to make a positive impact on your thinking. You can discover the power of managing your thoughts and making them work for you instead of against you.

Using the BWRT Emergency Stop technique

The changes you make to negative versus positive thinking can be empowering and long-lasting. It is worth trying for a few days to check in with your inner voice until dismissing old negative ways of talking to yourself becomes second nature.

Repetitive judgements your inner voice makes about yourself can create harsh negative judgements that you have attached to real-life events. This way of interpreting what happens to you as other negative judgements might require some additional leverage to resolve. I recommend you use a BWRT (Brian Wave Recursive Therapy[5]) technique called the Emergency Stop created by Terence Watts. While it is not as effective as an entire session of BWRT, it is a handy tool, helping you interrupt automatic, habitual negative judgements you make about events that you have experienced.

Here are the directions. When you are sure what to do, begin with your eyes closed:

Step 1: Imagine a clock face – an analogue clock with an hour hand, a minute hand and a second hand. The clock is working, and note you can see the second hand moving – make it vivid and authentic in your mind's eye. Think about the colour of the hands and the face and if there are numerals or markers.

Step 2: Now focus your mind on an event you have negatively judged and make that event as vivid as possible. When it is as striking as you can make it, zoom in quickly to what seems to be the essential part of what happened, the real nub of that memory.

Step 3: Now freeze that solid! Make it as though it's a 3D model frozen in time, in which you can move, but nothing else can. Be inside it looking out, rather than outside it looking in. Freeze it solid!

Step 4: Now see the clock face, and this time notice that the clock has stopped – the second hand isn't moving by even the tiniest amount. Focus on that clock that has stopped at that time, absolutely stopped and open your eyes as soon as you've focused on it.

What has happened to your negative feelings or judgements about the event you focused on? Are they less? Have they gone? You can repeat this technique if required or use it on any memories you have negatively judged.

Worksheet 5: Transforming your inner voice

Use this worksheet or your notebook to handwrite your reflections on your inner voice, including listing here all the things it says about you.

Key points to consider are:

- Consciously tune into your inner voice and assess if it's positive or negative.
- Discover your negative self-talk patterns and explore the possible origin of this negative voice.
- Interrupt and dismiss negative thoughts with the buzzer noise.
- Use EFT (page 93) to transform your negative self-talk.

6. Resolving unhelpful thinking styles

Are you losing sleep worrying about what might or might not happen?

Do your thoughts go around and around in your mind on an endless loop?

Does negative thinking spoil your enjoyment of life?

If you always feel anxious and plagued by worrying thoughts, it may be because you have developed an unhelpful thinking style. American psychiatrist Aaron Beck (1921–2021) was a professor in the department of psychiatry at the University of Pennsylvania, USA. He developed a theory about how your thinking style influences your thoughts and reactions to circumstances and events. Your thinking style can make a difference between feeling burdened by worry or being able to glide through life and never be overly concerned about anything. Perhaps you can recognise patterns in your thinking? These are specific 'cognitive distortions', or unhelpful ways of interpreting the world, that Beck identified.

Black-and-white thinking

'Black-and-white thinking' refers to seeing things in absolute, extreme categories. Things are all good or all bad in the black-and-white thinker's mindset.

This thinking pattern fails to account for nuance, complexity or middle ground. For example, a student who fails one test may see themselves as a total failure and 'stupid', forgetting the many tests they've passed with excellent marks. Or someone who argues with their partner once may see the relationship as 'completely broken' rather than an opportunity to communicate better in the future while still appreciating the good times.

Overgeneralisation

Overgeneralisation involves taking one instance, event or piece of evidence and making sweeping negative conclusions far beyond the current situation. A single failure becomes 'yet more proof' of an endless pattern of defeat in the mind of someone prone to overgeneralisation.

An example would be getting turned down for one job interview and concluding, 'I'm unemployable and will never get a job offer'. Or eating one piece of cake and thinking, 'I have no self-control; my diet is completely ruined, so I may as well binge eat now'.

Mental filter

Mental filtering refers to paying attention only to the negative details in a situation while ignoring or dismissing the positive. It's like a filter has been placed over reality, screening out anything good so that your world appears disproportionately gloomy. For instance, you received constructive feedback at work, with one area needing development noted while multiple strengths were also highlighted. The mental filter causes you to obsess solely over that one critical comment you received while failing to feel good about the positive feedback.

Disqualifying the positive

Disqualifying the positive, or 'positive discounting', involves brushing off our positive experiences, events or accomplishments as if they 'didn't count' for some reason. You maintain a negative belief even when faced with clear evidence.

An example would be finishing a major project ahead of the deadline and under budget and thinking it wasn't well done enough to be impressive or didn't make enough of a difference. Or completing a strenuous workout routine but telling yourself it was all too easy to count. Any success gets dismissed as a fluke or stroke of luck.

Jumping to conclusions

Jumping to conclusions means drawing negative interpretations or assumptions before reasonably evaluating a situation. There are two types:

1. Mind reading means believing you know what someone else is thinking (usually negatively) without adequate evidence to justify this belief. For

example, if your friend doesn't text back immediately, you immediately assume they must be mad at you.

2. Fortune-telling means pessimistically anticipating you know precisely how a future situation will turn out before it happens – such as just 'knowing' you will fail at a new task before even getting started.

Magnification and minimisation

Also called 'catastrophising', this distortion involves exaggerating the importance of insignificant negatives while minimising meaningful positives. You view events in your life selectively with a magnified lens over the bad stuff and a minimised lens over the good stuff – for example, making a significant mistake at work and believing you'll undoubtedly be fired while downplaying the significance of recently landing the company an important new client, or obsessing over an awkward five minutes of a two-hour first date that otherwise went wonderfully.

Emotional reasoning

Emotional reasoning makes you believe something must be true because you 'feel' it strongly rather than basing beliefs on evidence. Because it feels real, you assume it is accurate regardless of the facts – for instance, failing an exam might leave you feeling like a complete failure. You then conclude you must be stupid and incompetent based mainly on those intense negative feelings rather than your scores on previous exams or other evidence of ability.

'Should' statements

'Should' statements reflect rigid assumptions about how you, others or the world 'should' function. When reality fails to match these unreasonable expectations, you feel resentment, anger, frustration and sometimes shame. For example, you criticise yourself after the opening weekend of your small business for not immediately attracting droves of loyal customers ('I should have done better marketing...'), or you feel furious when a partner wants to change dinner plans at the last minute because your partner 'should just know' you don't like plan changes.

Labelling

Labelling means attaching an often unreasonable, extreme label to yourself or others without considering nuance or mitigating factors. Rather than saying, 'I made a mistake' it becomes, 'I'm an idiot' in your mind.

Applying such unhelpful labels fuels feelings of anger, inadequacy and hopelessness and prevents personal growth. And labelling others in this way ('Jim is so lazy!') damages relationships and feeds into more distorted thinking.

Personalisation

Personalisation centres around blaming yourself for something you are not responsible for — essentially taking everything personally. Events around you seem explicitly directed at or caused directly by you, even when there's no factual reason to draw this conclusion – for example, believing a friend hanging back from inviting you to their party must be doing so because you did something to offend them versus considering more likely reasons; or feeling that random bad events, like suddenly needing your car towed, happened solely to ruin your day.

Identifying your thinking style

Identifying what thinking style or the mix of thinking styles is your default setting is one of the first steps to taking conscious control of your thoughts so that you are no longer a passive casualty of your thinking imperatives. Psychologists consider these types of thinking styles to be disordered thinking, meaning your thoughts subconsciously determine your emotions. You may have developed these thinking styles over time, and it has come to feel natural for you to think this way. Still, you can see how they negatively influence your mood and how you feel about yourself. When considering what kind of thinker you may be, it's also helpful to explore whose thinking style your own reminds you of. For instance, were one or both of your parents catastrophic or black-and-white thinkers? If so, that can influence your thinking style. Once you can identify, 'Oh, my father was always a worrier or an over-thinker', then you begin to make a space or create boundaries around your thoughts so that when you slip into worrying, you can consciously say to yourself, 'I'm just thinking the same way my dad always did, and I don't want to do that anymore.'

Insights like these can help you choose to interrupt your thinking and let it go consciously. Changing a thinking style will take vigilance and insight. With practice, you can have a thought; decide whether it's helpful, interrupt it, and formulate a more helpful positive alternative opinion instead.

How to change the way you think

Unhelpful thinking styles involve you focusing on the negatives in any given situation and ignoring any positives, which can cause significant increases in your stress levels. The unhelpful styles I've described above are forms of cognitive distortion or disorganised thinking. Left unchallenged, they become your entrenched way of viewing the world. Imagine a seed in the palm of your hand. When you water the seed, it begins to sprout and rapidly grows into a mighty and all-enveloping vine from that initial green shoot. Now imagine the seed represents a negative thought, and the water you pour on it represents the attention you pay to reinforce it. Very soon, the negative or catastrophic thinking has grown so huge that it surrounds you just like a tangled vine from the seed. The vine twines suffocatingly around you, filling where you are from floor to ceiling and wall to wall. Thoughts allowed to develop in this way dominate in an unhelpful way and take all the available oxygen until they become all you can think about.

Pause and breathe

When you realise that you are blowing things out of all proportion, it is essential to pause and take a breath or two to help you to gain a more balanced perspective. Suppressing your breathing happens without your realising it. When caught up in catastrophic thinking, your breathing becomes much more shallow.

An effective way to change your thoughts is to assess your breathing by taking three gentle in and out breaths. Score your depth of breathing on a scale of zero to 10 by taking an intuitive guess. A zero score means no breath in your body, and a score of 10 signifies breathing deeply, freely and fully.

You may be surprised to find your breathing is below a five. To increase the depth of your breathing, you can tap with a soft fist around your collarbone and focus on breathing more deeply for a few moments. Tapping around your collarbone is part of EFT (page 93) and can help you feel more grounded and secure.

Reaching out to touch the collarbone is a natural response for many people when they hear bad news. It's an instinctive, self-comforting reaction. You can use it to move from negative thinking to feeling calmer and more stable.

When you are stressed, and your breathing becomes restricted and shallow, it can be challenging to identify any positives. In reality, very few situations are without some merit, however slender. I look at the role of breathing and stress reduction more fully on page 101 and show you how to overcome this typical stress response.

Thinking outside of the box

When something has happened that has profound and far-reaching repercussions in your life – it could be a health crisis, losing your job or the breakdown of a valued relationship – what if you are experiencing a situation that feels legitimately catastrophic? Something that feels momentous, whatever way you look at it. At times like this, it is easy to fall into ruminative, circular thinking, so it is crucial to gain some perspective instead of spiralling further and further down into negativity and even depression.

In your mind, visualise a courtroom scene to explore your catastrophic conclusion. Just like a barrister, present the evidence for and against your thoughts and ask yourself what you can learn from being in this situation. It can be helpful even to pretend it is someone else going through this experience, not you. Ask yourself how you would advise a person in this situation. Although you may have little compassion and empathy for yourself, you may find you can be kinder and more rational on behalf of someone else. Role-playing can help you look at a situation from a different angle, and you may feel more resourceful and less overwhelmed when you remove yourself from the equation.

Don't forget to be vigilant and interrupt yourself if caught in the suffocating tangle of possible consequences and outcomes. Instead, focusing on what you, or another person, could learn from this adverse situation is helpful. You can then use your insights to feel more resilient and help overcome the challenges you face.

Finally, if you struggle to see beyond your negative thinking, ask someone you trust for their opinion. Use their perspective on your situation to help give you clarity. Hopefully, they can show you the problem is more nuanced than you initially believed from your unhelpful thinking style.

Breaking state

'Breaking state' is purposely doing something to interrupt your thinking and to stop your negative, ruminating, circular thoughts. So, instead of submitting to hours of negative thinking, doing something physical is the best way to break state. In Energy Therapy, there is a well-established technique called 'cross crawl', where you stand up and alternate raising your left knee to tap that knee with your right hand and then lower that knee and raise your right knee and tap it with your left hand. Repeat five to 10 times.

Alternatively, if you are able to, you can run upstairs or go outside in the fresh air. You need to break the negative thinking pattern and stop allowing your thoughts to dictate your feelings.

Applying the century rule

For those prone to immediately assuming the worst when faced with adversity, catastrophic thinking can feel like an automatic trap that is impossible to avoid. In the moment, as anxiety spikes and your mind races to only the most dire 'what ifs', it seems you have no power to redirect your thoughts in a more balanced, realistic direction. In these instances of getting hijacked by catastrophising fears, it becomes vital to have 'shock tactics' that act like a mental emergency brake. These disruptive techniques reorient your brain from the anxious emotional mud it's stuck in to gain a rational perspective.

One such highly effective shock tactic is the 'century rule'. When you notice those catastrophic thoughts and 'end of the world' feelings swirling as a setback occurs, pause and deliberately ask yourself: 'Will this likely impact or matter to me in 100 years?'

Consider what a tiny blip even five years is in your life, let alone a century. The intensity of most conflicts, mistakes, arguments or grief naturally mellows with time and distance, even just months later.

Apply the century rule to whatever situation triggers present fears and anxieties — query how significant this will seem with long-range hindsight.

This line of questioning acts like a mental and emotional palate cleanser, clearing short-term overreactions to reveal actuality. It starkly contrasts the urgency emotions would have you believe exists now from this temporary hardship or pain.

With some separation, you recognise that anything rarely sends your whole life irreversibly off course overnight. How you respond, learn and realign going forward remains within your power. Reframing struggles through a century-long time horizon lends perspective and patience for the next best steps.

Learning that 'this too will pass' doesn't invalidate present discomfort. It does, however, help to avoid making major panic-based overcorrections that can worsen situations. You can centre yourself enough to respond thoughtfully.

Over time and through repetition of practising the century rule, you quickly activate that mental handbrake early when destructive thoughts accelerate. No longer entirely so imprisoned by emotions, wisdom broadens your vision to address any size of hardship. Just asking, 'Where will this fit given the long arc of life?' grants freedom to act from vision rather than visceral reaction.

Breaking the cycle

Much scientific research on resilience focuses on cultivating children's ability to bounce back from adversity. However, what if your family circumstances were not conducive to your developing resilience in your childhood?

Awareness is the first step to building resilience and owning your life. Here are four common unhelpful behaviours you may recognise you demonstrate in adulthood that may have their origin in your childhood. Bear in mind there is no such thing as a straightforward correlation of cause and effect here. As to your family dynamics, you must consider many subtle and not-so-subtle factors you experienced growing up. See if any of the following examples resonate with you. Be prepared for insights and a-ha moments of recognition.

1. Do you find it hard to make decisions and motivate yourself to get on?

Do you believe your self-motivation difficulties are due to you being micro-managed as a child? Also, if you lived with constant correction and criticism in childhood, it can make it difficult for you as an adult to develop trust in your decision-making abilities.

'Helicopter parenting' is a growing trend where parents closely oversee their children's every move. This can include taking complete control of their school projects and homework assignments. While it's natural for parents to offer assistance, taking charge to the point where the work is no longer their child's is not beneficial. The desire to micro-manage is often a result of a parent's insecurities and anxieties manifesting through their children's lives. Helicopter parenting is now recognised as a negative parenting style and is thought to reflect society's reported increase in overall anxiety.

Micro-management of a child's behaviour can undoubtedly play a part in raising adults who struggle with self-motivation. However, what is even more likely to inhibit self-motivation is the unambiguous message that controlling parents often convey to their children. The family dynamic frequently expressed is that parental love and acceptance by either one parent, or both, is conditional and intrinsically linked with their child's ability to comply with their wishes.

Parents do not necessarily demonstrate negative controlling behaviour conspicuously. As a child, you probably quickly learnt to pick up your parents' subtle signals of how you must behave to be accepted and loved by them. To a young child, their parents are all-powerful. A parent's disapproval of their child is often unspoken. When one or both parents withdraw positive regard, love and acceptance, it can be subtly expressed with a raised eyebrow, a cut of the eye, or a face turned away. It doesn't need to be a physical blow for the child to feel devastated.

The more control the parents demonstrate and the more demanding of conformity they are can leave the child with no choice but to unconsciously surrender their own emotional needs to the imperatives of their parents. As a child, your first drive is to survive, and to do this, and you would attempt to guarantee your parents' favourable attitude towards you, whatever the emotional cost.

If you were raised with high levels of negative judgement and pressure to conform, it is not surprising that, as an adult, you try hard to comply with the wishes of other people around you. Feeling undermined could make you in adulthood doubt who you are or what you authentically want for yourself. You may well habitually prioritise other people's needs over and above your own. Could this be you?

2. Procrastination and distraction

Adults who procrastinate to the extent that they are sabotaging their life can be rebelling against how they were parented as a child. A small body of research undertaken by Esther Rothblum and her team in the 1980s suggested that children with overly critical, demanding parents might choose not to learn tasks to avoid failure.[6] Further research in the 1990s by Professor Gordon Flett and his colleagues concluded that procrastination might be a child's response to the expectation that their parents will respond in a harsh and controlling manner to what they can achieve.[7]

Research does seem to show that having experienced an authoritarian parenting style can negatively influence self-motivation. Having too great a parental investment riding on a child's innate ability can harm their development and wellbeing. Equally, the reverse situation, where a child is raised in a household with little or no interest in what they could achieve, has disadvantages. Interestingly, in Flett's study, children who rated their parents as having high demands for control but who also demonstrated warmth and responsiveness in these relationships reported a lower level of procrastination.

Great expectations and hot housing

Some children are constantly pushed to achieve and put under immense pressure to fulfil their parent's expectations. This can include what is known as 'hot housing', when parents prioritise providing specialist tutors, residential summer schools and other such 'support'. If you were raised in this way, you might attribute your success to your parents' high expectations. However, not everyone who was expected as a child to be a high achiever fulfils their potential and lives life as a well-balanced, well-rounded adult. Clients who come to me struggling with chronic procrastination were often raised in families with either excessive or extremely low levels of expectation. Many adults raised under the oppressive expectation of their parents struggle to find traction in their own life once the pushing has stopped and become overly passive as their own motivation never had the opportunity to develop.

A second family dynamic is where your parents ignored you as a child, overlooked you or made you feel stupid or flawed. You may have had parents who put you down instead of elevating you. If you were raised with constant criticism, this could often reflect how your parents were parented. Equally, they could have experienced parents or carers who had little or no interest or commitment in them achieving anything in their life.

These two examples of parenting style are the extreme points on the spectrum and, of course, many sub-divisions exist in between. So, an illustration of this might be if you, as a child, were raised by parents who made you feel that you only deserved their love if you kept practising the violin, made the football team, or won the spelling B. It could encourage you to grow up to believe your intrinsic value and sense of self-worth is not who you are but what you can do. On the other hand, if you as a child were over-looked by your parents who were unable to recognise your unique qualities, you might have tried very hard to get your parents' attention by behaving well or equally by misbehaving.

The extremes of both parenting styles distort the ideal situation of you growing to fulfil your full potential while being loved and valued for who you are. Does this resonate with you?

3. Do you prefer to be in control but feel conflicted about making decisions?

If you behave in a controlling way as an adult, you were most likely overly controlled by your parents or caregivers in your childhood. You will have mimicked the behaviour you experienced from an early age, and it may feel like it is entirely normal for you. Having felt powerless or disrespected as a child, you will also have witnessed how dominating and bullying behaviour was effective for other people to get what they wanted. This can make a controlling character trait seem appealing to you. Also, so great would be your drive to avoid being controlled in your adult life you may have chosen a career path where you can more or less guarantee to be in control. A career as a police officer or joining the military may seem appealing.

However, if you have a deeper insight, you may recognise your childhood experiences have contributed to making you the kind of leader who people describe as an 'impatient boss', a 'dismissive' or 'critical teacher', or an 'emotionally disconnected CEO'. You may also have subconsciously chosen people in your life who you thought you could dominate, manipulate, bully or nag, and that dynamic might be replicated many times over in different areas of your life.

You may have only recently realised the detrimental effects of your controlling tendencies when those in a close relationship with you express their unhappiness with your behaviour. Some people's controlling tendencies can be so extreme that those close to them have said it feels abusive and damages the relationship.

The irony of being raised in a controlling family dynamic is that, once you become an adult, it can feel emotionally challenging to step into your power and make decisions for yourself. There can often be the dynamic of wanting to be in control and then feeling hugely uncomfortable making decisions and agonising over whether you've made the right choice when you finally decide something. Does that sound familiar to you? It's not surprising when your parents or adult carers focus so much on telling you what to do rather than teaching you how to work things out and decide for yourself.

The long-awaited autonomy of adulthood, where you can, in theory, do almost whatever you want with your life, can lead to overthinking and time-consuming self-doubt. It can feel as though, having finally made it to adulthood, you have graduated to being in control of your life without being equipped with the emotional tools to make sound decisions or take decisive action. Without the opportunity in childhood to learn through the experience of making your own mistakes in a supportive family, it can leave you with a deficit in resilience. The ability to be resilient and bounce back from disappointments and mistakes enables adults to take healthy risks without the incapacitating fear of negative consequences. Do any of these behaviours feel familiar to you?

4. Are you a people pleaser, always on high alert for how others feel?

If you felt unsafe in your family or unsure of where you stood with your adult carers, you may well have developed sophisticated and subtle strategies to stay under the radar to keep yourself out of trouble. You will have learnt from an early age to be hyper-vigilant, on the lookout for mood swings or impending bursts of anger in your environment. In this way, you hoped to deflect or minimise any negative behaviour directed at you. To do this, you will have become adept at people pleasing and put the emotional needs of others over and above your own. This strategy will be one you developed when, as a child, you had few resources to draw upon other than endeavouring to blend in as much as possible.

Taking this well-practised behaviour into adulthood means you can be a chameleon in your behaviour as you shift and adapt to subordinate your emotional needs while prioritising the needs of those around you. Chronic people pleasers often have an underdeveloped sense of their own intuitive needs due to never being encouraged to honour their authentic selves.

If as a child you developed people-pleasing behaviour, it may be because you were raised in a challenging home environment run by controlling, bullying

[go to page 74]

Worksheet 6: Changing your thinking style

Use the worksheet or your notebook to handwrite your intentions here and the new behaviours you want to embed as habits for the future.

Key points to consider are:

- How are you actively demonstrating kindness and compassion to yourself on a daily basis?
- Revive activities this week you've stopped doing that previously brought you joy.
- Reconnect with caring friends; human connection is key to sound mental health.
- Explore your values, goals and passions to remind yourself what motivates you.

[Cont'd from page 71]

or narcissistic adults. The irony is that you may well be attracted in your adult life to dominating, manipulative people who exhibit the same behaviours as your parents or main caregivers. People pleasers also find it hard to set healthy boundaries for themselves. With low self-esteem, it is almost impossible to prioritise self-care. An inability to say no to the demands of others, however outlandish or however it may impact your wellbeing, is an easy gauge of how much of a people pleaser you are. Perceived failure to meet your impossibly high, self-imposed standards of perfection leads to feelings of shame and guilt. Your anxiety is also increased as your negative self-talk insists you are only of value to others if you are being taken advantage of or exploited by them. Combined in this toxic mix of behaviour and its consequences are feelings of responsibility for the happiness and wellbeing of others over and above your own.

Change is possible

There are many more childhood dynamics than those I've highlighted here, which are prone to be transferred to adult dynamics. How you behave can be changed or modified to make you think and feel differently about yourself and your relationships with others. Just because you recognise a blueprint from childhood doesn't mean you are condemned to live in ways that do not bring you happiness or fulfilment. First, focus on the insights and the a-ha moments; only by understanding your childhood's dynamic and the coping strategies you developed in response can you break the pattern.

Fortunately, once you recognise negative behaviour in yourself, resolving the issues from your childhood is possible. With that comes the opportunity to change how you behave and relate to others, which can improve your life on many levels. Even though the adolescent brain may provide the most fertile ground for change, resilience building is not limited to youth. Research has shown that adults of whatever age can take steps to leave their childhood limitations, and even early trauma, behind them by enhancing their resilience.

Building resilience cannot occur in isolation and requires people to interact with, create and build relationships, explore cultural traditions, and more. Every opportunity you have to witness resilience in others allows you to increase your own. One of the most potent ways to improve resilience is to model it.

7. How to implement change

Changes in how you think and feel about yourself can come as cathartic breakthroughs or subtle, incremental steps that free you from the stranglehold of your past. Here are actionable steps to change how you think and feel about yourself to become more resilient in the present.

1. Being kind to yourself is at the heart of all personal development and change work

If your internal dialogue is one of critical, negative judgements, it will be very challenging to feel positive about yourself. I explain the steps you need to take to turn off and transform your inner voice on page 51. Achieving this is life-changing, so don't skip those instructions, and implement the steps as soon as possible.

2. Revisit what has made you happy and do it again now

Did you once love dancing, paddle boarding, or singing in a choir? Did you participate in any activity you've now dropped from your life? We all live hectic and pressured lives, so it's easy to drop the activities that feed our souls.

Take a few moments to scan your memories to remind yourself of past activities that brought you joy. Your inner negative voice will quickly tell you, 'Oh yes, I used to love swimming, but I was thinner then', or 'I used to love to dance, but I was younger then'. Dismiss these limiting beliefs for the unhelpful thoughts they are and start deciding how you can bring these sources of pleasure back into your life. Start small if doing these things in the outside world feels too much. Dance in your living room. Sing in the shower. Start and set the intention to be courageous so that now, or in the not too distant future, you will walk out again poolside for a swimming session or find a local choir you can join and feel the inner satisfaction of your own and all those other voices singing together in harmony.

3. Have you been an unreliable friend and now rarely socialise?

Supportive friends understand and value you for your personality and character. If you've been out of touch for a while with people who you know care about you and who you value, then you are denying yourself a source of enriching human interaction. Humans thrive on positive connections with other people. The pressured way we live can challenge finding and maintaining a relationship with like-minded people. Having a network of positive, supportive friends and relatives in your life can improve your wellbeing in many ways, including perhaps extending your life.

A study into social relationships and health published in the journal *Science* in 1988 established strong empirical evidence for a link between social relationships and health.[8] Studies consistently show an increased risk of premature death among people with limited, sometimes low-quality, social relationships. Studies of humans and animals also suggest that social isolation is a major risk factor for mortality from widely varying causes.

Considering this study, what can you do to improve your social relationships? You could try some of these suggestions:

- **Start saying yes instead of no.** When invited to an event, go along instead of saying no and staying at home. Going out and socialising can become a habit just as much as staying in. It just takes you to step outside your comfort zone to change.
- **Get back in touch with people you haven't seen in a while.** Call or text people you've been out of touch with to see if they'd like to meet up. Maybe suggest an activity or a place you used to go to together when you were last in contact. Apologise for being out of touch. People are generally quite forgiving of others' failings, and if they are genuine friends, they would be more than willing to meet up with you again.
- **Be reliable from now onwards.** If you say you are going to do something or have arranged to meet someone, you must follow through on your promise. You may have gained a reputation amongst your friends for being unreliable and cancelling commitments you've made at the last minute. Equally, people may have judged your past antisocial attitude and decided you are stand-

offish and not interested in being friends with them.

- **Demonstrate that you are reliable.** You may have to build bridges with people before they accept your commitment to being a reliable friend. You can talk with them about your past flakey tendencies and apologise for being unreliable. However, you will make a more significant impression by demonstrating that you have changed your behaviour by building a track record of being dependable and showing up as promised.
- **Think about who drains and who builds your energy.** Fine-tune your radar to identify so-called friends or acquaintances who make you feel deflated or exhausted after being in their company. They are most likely not supportive friendships and could reinforce old abusive behaviour patterns.

Your goal is to build a mutually supportive network of friends around you and be open to experiencing the benefits of feeling less isolated. Not only will this help bolster your self-esteem but you will discover how being a good friend to others improves your sense of wellbeing too.

Strategies to build resilience

Having explored the family dynamics outlined in this book, you may recognise you were not raised in the most advantageous way to build resilience in your childhood. You may acknowledge that in the past, you needed to be preoccupied with surviving the challenging circumstances of your early years. The good news is that strategies to build resilience can be learnt later in life. These strategies can help you trust your judgement, put healthy boundaries in place and feel self-compassion so that you treat yourself with kindness, honouring your unique qualities.

Connect to your intuition

Intuition refers to having an inner knowing or 'gut feeling' that guides you. It's when you get a hunch or inkling about something that feels meaningful. Intuition is your inner voice communicating wisdom to help direct decisions. For example, you meet someone new and instantly feel distrustful without knowing why. Or you consider applying for a job and have an intuitive sense it would make you unhappy in the long run despite the high pay. That strong inner radar is your intuition sending you signals.

Developing a strong sense of intuition leads to feeling empowered and confident in your judgement. You can act in alignment with your inner truth, even if you can't logically explain the reasons. You trust those gut reactions to risks or opportunities.

Without reliable intuition, people often feel confused, indecisive and unable to explain their choices. Ignoring intuition can lead us into situations that leave us burned out, miserable and regretful despite seeming logically 'correct' at the time.

An underdeveloped sense of intuition is common for adults who were not encouraged to tune into their emotions as children. Growing up, you likely learned to ignore your instincts and needs if your preferences and insights were frequently dismissed or overridden. Rebuilding trust in your inner wisdom takes practice but provides huge lifelong rewards.

Psychologists recognise that developing intuition strengthens self-trust and resilience. Rather than feeling life randomly happens to you, intuition helps you feel in the driver's seat. An inner light would guide you rather than feeling you are tossing about aimlessly.

Start noticing when you have a 'knowing' about something – that's your intuition communicating. Acting on these instincts and taking note of the results builds confidence to heed those inner prompts increasingly.

Locus of control: influence over life direction

People with what psychologists call an 'external locus of control' believe they have little power over achieving their ambitions or directing their life path. It's as if they feel buffeted about by external winds with no agency. In contrast, people with a so-called 'internal locus of control' have the perspective that they can influence outcomes and make intentional choices. They have self-efficacy – that is, the belief that their actions have an impact. Unsurprisingly, those with an internal locus of control tend to feel more hopeful and persistent in pursuing their goals.

Having an external locus of control frequently stems from growing up in an environment that discourages confidence in one's thinking. Without caregivers emphasising the development of self-trust, intuition and an internal locus of control, these skills remain underdeveloped.

The good news is you can consciously cultivate these resilience-building life skills at any age. It simply takes commitment through actionable steps.

Assessing your intuition

On a scale from one to 10, how would you rate the strength of intuition (with 10 being the highest)? Take a moment to reflect.

The ideal level is 10, but any lower score means you have room for growth. Have compassion for yourself if your intuition feels muted or unreliable. You can strengthen this skill over time by taking small but consistent steps to tune into, document and act from your inner knowing.

Sometimes, those with an under-developed sense of internal empowerment attempt to mute their limited intuition even further through unhealthy coping habits like overeating, drinking too much or smoking. This behaviour helps explain the high occurrence of addiction issues among populations struggling with low self-esteem and past trauma. Rather than feeling that uncomfortable inner radar warning them against something and choosing to listen to it, it becomes easier to override the cautionary flag altogether through quick-fix numbing mechanisms. But this comes at a grave cost to physical and mental health.

Others override their intuition through stimulation-seeking behaviours like excessive caffeine intake or stress-induced adrenaline rushes. You may push past exhaustion through hyperactivity or sleep deprivation, ignoring what your body tells you it needs for restoration.

In all cases, the tragedy is that your inner wisdom trying to send you essential signals gets dismissed as irrelevant background noise. But that connection to your intuition and taking appropriate action is vital to resilience.

Simple steps to expand intuition

The good news is everyone can rebuild their relationship with their intuition through simple, consistent daily steps:

1. Carve out quiet time for reflection. Even just 5-10 minutes a day without distractions tunes you into inner guidance.
2. Notice gut reactions and document them. What subtle instincts or hesitations do you brush aside? Journaling these helps discern meaningful patterns over time.
3. Thank your intuition. Express gratitude when hesitancy prevents something undesirable. This positive reinforcement breeds trust.
4. Experiment with acting counter to intuition. Note that going against those instincts leads to poor consequences.

In all these ways, you ultimately relearn to discern and amplify the quiet inner signals attempting to guide you. As your intuition reconnects to conscious awareness, you no longer need to override it with harmful mechanisms. Instead, you feel increasingly steadied by this inner compass directing you towards health and purpose.

Developing intuition forges resilience

In many ways, intuition provides the guiding force for developing other resilience-building mindsets and skills. You clarify values guiding major life decisions by tuning into your inner wisdom. By documenting when acting on hesitations leads to better outcomes, self-trust grows. That self-trust transfers to having faith in your ability to handle life's inevitable ups and downs.

Rather than feeling you have little control amidst external forces, intuition helps guide you through life's complexities. It becomes second nature to catch, interpret and respond to intuitive cues with practice. That allows proactive navigation, staying aligned to your authentic self rather than feeling buffeted aimlessly, at the mercy of luck or circumstance.

So, in daily quiet moments, begin rebuilding rapport with your intuition. A lifelong friend awaits, ready to provide support, discernment and comfort whenever you need it. Reclaim this inner lifeline today.

Additional benefits of a strong intuition

Aside from promoting self-trust and resilience, developing your intuition provides myriad other concrete benefits to your health, relationships and sense of purpose.

Firstly, several research studies have provided evidence for the benefits of intuition in reducing anxiety and stress. For example, a study by Voss and colleagues (2017) found that intuitive decision making was associated with lower levels of anxiety and higher levels of self-efficacy and satisfaction.[9] Similarly, a study by Sinclair and Ashkanasy (2005) found that intuitive managers reported less stress and more positive emotions than analytical managers.[10] These findings suggest that tapping into one's inner wisdom can facilitate confident and effective actions, rather than being paralysed by doubt and uncertainty.

Intuition helps you to manage feeling overwhelmed by providing a clear inner ranking of priorities aligned with your authentic values. Without relying on intuition, you risk constantly reacting to external pressures rather than purposefully moving towards what matters most.

Your relationships also improve as you set needs-based boundaries guided by inner knowing. Rather than resentments festering through ignoring internal misgivings, you communicate something that feels intuitively 'off' to you more effectively. That prevents guessing games or behaving inauthentically.

Additionally, intuitive nudges can lead you to serendipitous opportunities at unexpected times. Paying attention means you pick up on signals pointing you towards growth possibilities that logic alone would miss. Many creative epiphanies originate from intuitive bursts we then build upon.

So, ultimately, the case for developing your intuition rests upon the reality that it guides you home to who you authentically are. It steers you towards self-care and alignment with your values no matter how far you wander off track under outside demands. By learning its language, you progress confidently through calm and chaotic periods, staying rooted within.

Rebuilding intuition takes patience and compassion

Like any new skill, rebuilding intuition after years of distrust takes gentle patience with yourself as progress unfolds slowly. Have compassion for the younger you who adapted to override inner wisdom for survival at the time. Realise now you get to write a new script for your life moving forward.

Aim for consistency with daily intuitive practices rather than pressuring quick results overnight. Consider working with a counsellor trained in mind-body modalities to accelerate your progress if needed. Many kinds of compassionate guides exist to help you reconnect with what was always innately within you. You deserve to reclaim and unwind this relationship with your inner voice.

So, in times of turbulence, pause and listen for inner steadiness rising beneath the surface chaos. Your intuition awaits patiently to centre and direct you. The journey back to yourself begins in quiet trust today.

Ways to strengthen your intuition

1. The ritual of writing Morning Pages

In the self-development book, *The Artist's Way*, the author, Julia Cameron, includes this powerful way to explore your thoughts. The book was originally written for artists and other creative professionals who were experiencing a creative crisis. Over 25 years old now, Julia's classic and its processes have helped many people from all walks of life to discover their inner dialogue or get back onto their creative path and live their life more authentically. The exercise she calls the Morning Pages requires you to fill three sides of A4 with handwritten words as the first thing you do every morning. Write whatever comes into your head, and don't stop until you've filled the requisite pages. Most importantly, these are your words, just for you and not for sharing. Julia's other guideline is that you don't read back through them for several weeks to avoid allowing your ego to be its judgemental, negative self.

Some days, writing your Morning Pages will feel banal, and the whole act will feel like drudgery, while on other days, you will find the process is filled with insights and a-ha moments. Stick at it for at least a month, and you'll find it a valued and satisfying part of getting to know yourself.

2. The gift of saying no

For many women, disappointing others is something they strive to avoid. It can be challenging to refuse requests from loved ones, such as giving up free time or taking on additional tasks. This tendency may stem from societal expectations that girls should be compliant and accommodating from a young age. In some instances, girls may even receive praise for prioritising others' needs over their own, while boys generally learn to prioritise their own needs. However, learning to say 'No' can be empowering and essential to caring for yourself. It may take some practice to become comfortable with the idea, but saying 'No' can be a revolutionary act that leads to greater self-care and personal fulfilment.

When asked to do something you're unsure about, check in with yourself first instead of agreeing with a knee-jerk 'Yes' response. Take a breath and pause. What's the hunch you feel about this? Hunches or gut feelings come from your intuition, which always has your higher good in mind. If your hunch says 'No,' then use the 'stuck record technique' below to ensure you don't get pressured to do things you don't want to do.

Use the stuck record technique when asked to do something your gut tells you you don't want to do. Say, in your own words, something like, 'Oh, I wish I could, but I just can't'. Repeat the short phrase just like a stuck record. With this approach, you don't explain yourself or expand upon your chosen words. Eventually, your 'No' will be acknowledged.

Start small. Think of your ability to say 'No' like a muscle – the more you use your muscles, the stronger they get and the more you say 'No', the more comfortable you become turning down requests that sap your energy and use up so much of your time. Imagine only choosing to do what you want and being led by your intuition. If something good comes from this gift, it could be life-enhancing.

3. Taking time to pause

Mindfulness is the practice of intentionally bringing your entire presence and awareness to the current moment rather than getting carried away in worries about the future or regrets over the past. It means gently noticing thoughts and sensations without getting tangled up in them. Pausing throughout the day to take mindful breaks can help you gain perspective when you notice your mind spiralling into over-analysis or excessive concern. Rather than following frenetic thoughts down the rabbit hole, these moments of stillness allow you to redirect your attention to the present consciously.

You can build more mindful pauses into your routine when walking, cooking, brushing your teeth or doing other daily activities. The key is fully arriving at the action without multi-tasking or allowing the constant inner mental chatter to dominate. Many mental health professionals confirm that mindful walking allows people to tap into inner wisdom and stability that gets drowned out by perpetual busyness. The rhythm of walking calmly grounds you in the present while enabling reflection.

Unlike meditating with eyes closed, mindful walking permits you to consciously take in your surroundings with all your senses while tuning inward. You give equal focus to the external environment and your inner landscape. This style of moving with self-awareness boosts confidence by allowing you to identify and sit with thoughts and feelings you previously suppressed or avoided. By repeatedly returning attention gently to the present, you realise you can interrupt thought patterns rather than fuse with them.

Over time, mindful walking encourages you to observe your thoughts non-judgementally as they come to you. This practice leads to an enhanced ability to regulate where you place your focus and decreases reactivity. Rather than feeling like a helpless victim of endless rumination, you strengthen skills to pivot your concentration towards what truly matters. Mindfulness plants you firmly in the driver's seat of your inner world.

4. What are your dreams for?

While you sleep, your subconscious mind processes and stores new information, memories, emotions, stress and trauma. REM (rapid eye movement) phases happen in the latter part of your sleep cycles, each of which takes between 70-100 minutes (early in the night) and 90-120 minutes (later in the night), so you should go through four to six cycles per night. That means, four to six periods of REM sleep, with these getting longer as the night progresses. During REM sleep, your eyes move rapidly behind closed eyelids, and your brain waves become more variable. This is when you dream.

Although dreams may seem like a convoluted narrative mixed with metaphors and symbols, their primary function seems to be to process emotions. While some parts of a dream may provide insight, most dreams are lost from conscious awareness upon waking.

Getting uninterrupted, long periods of sleep is crucial for mental wellbeing as it allows for periods of REM within cycles. Sleep deprivation, however, can cause extreme confusion and exhaustion and deny you the ability to experience REM sleep, essential for memory consolidation and other mental health functions.

It's worth noting that alcohol consumption always suppresses REM sleep and certain anxiety and depression medications may do so too, inhibiting the subconscious mind's ability to process emotions.

5. Achieve flow

Singing, dancing, drawing, sewing or knitting are all ways that can help you achieve flow. There are many other activities too that can do this for you. Being in a state of flow is forgetting external distractions and being fully present in the moment of now. You become engrossed in an activity and inaccessible to external concerns and worries. During these states of flow, when time stands still, you are most receptive to insights, a-ha moments and new ideas as you are free of the wider world's white noise and general hum. These times could be when you are most open to listening to your intuition.

Face reality: The Stockdale paradox

The story of Pandora's box in Greek mythology was created to answer the profound philosophical question: Why do the gods allow bad things to happen to mortals, including sickness and death?

Pandora's myth describes how Zeus, the father of gods and men, collaborated with the other gods to set a trap for humans in revenge for Prometheus, who had tricked the gods and stolen their ability to create fire, giving this secret to mortals. Zeus ordered that a beautiful woman be moulded from the Earth and then presented to Prometheus's brother, Epimetheus.

Pandora was given a sealed earthenware jar, or a carved box depending on which version of the story one refers to, as her parting gift from the gods and told never to break the seal and open it. Once living on Earth, it wasn't long before her curiosity about what might be in the container became unbearable. When she could bear it no longer, she opened it in secret. Immediately, out flew every conceivable plague, sickness, death and many other evils which were released into the world for the first time. Realising her mistake, she slammed the box shut as quickly as she could, but the damage was done and would prove to be irreversible forever.

By closing the lid when she did, she managed to trap hope inside the box. The idea that hope was included in Pandora's box by the gods has sparked many a philosophical debate over the centuries. Many believe living in hope keeps them going forward in the face of great adversity, while others believe relying on hope can keep them entrapped in hopeless situations.

Redefining 'hope' as an active word

In everyday language, we often treat 'hope' as a passive state, referring to it as something fragile we either have or don't have. 'I've lost all hope,' we might say, or 'My hopes were dashed'. This usage depicts hope as something we cannot influence. However, psychologists concerned with resilience emphasise the importance of viewing hope instead as an active state with hope involving ongoing effort and movement towards creating possibilities rather than just wishfully, passively waiting.

So, instead of passively saying, 'I hope my business succeeds', with active hoping it becomes, 'I will hope my business succeeds through diligent planning, bold pitching to clients, and resilient iterations'. The latter centres on how you actively do something. This contrasts with perceiving hope as some external force judging your worthiness to receive a desired outcome passively. As an action word, centred on effort, hope lives within character – your grit to actively leverage all within reach to progress.

Even the most difficult circumstances contain overlooked openings only visible once old, rigid narratives loosen. Genuine hope centres on tenaciously finding those possibilities rather than expecting outside intervention. An active hope mindset powers the perseverance needed to create growth conditions however you're able.

Here are three examples of active hope and how intentional doing is centrally crucial for resilience.

1. Job searching: Rather than passively hoping to find a job, take concrete steps like updating your resume, networking, applying to openings, and preparing for interviews. Focus on the actions you can take to make yourself a strong candidate.
2. Developing a skill: Instead of hoping to someday improve at something, carve out time to actively practise it. Whether learning an instrument or a language, focus on the satisfaction that will come from persistence and achieving milestones.
3. Managing finances: Don't just hope for more savings, but make a budget to spend consciously and look for ways to increase income. Focus on how financial discipline now will enable freedom later.

However long the odds, retaining initiative generates tipping points. With an empowered, tenacious hope mindset centered on the 'how' – how you can proactively shift circumstances – you engineer solutions even when the odds seem long. This locomotive force of forward momentum contrasts with perceiving hope as a weakened state of wishing that external factors will resolve everything. Actionable hope drives change.

Hope is a 'doing' word

I want to explain the advantages of seeing hope in this way and adopting a different, more resilient perspective. The story of the late Vice Admiral James Stockdale is one of the most potent illustrations I've found of how living in passive hope can be a trap that not only potentially harms you but can, in extreme situations, lead to despair and premature death.

Stockdale was a US military officer held captive for over seven years during the Vietnam War in what was cynically nicknamed the 'Hanoi Hotel'. As the highest-ranking officer to be captured by the Vietcong, he was made an example of by his captors, who tortured him more than 20 times. Stockdale was not encouraged to believe he would survive the infamous prison and get to see his wife again, and yet, he had remarkable faith in the unknowable and never lost belief during his ordeal. He never questioned whether he would eventually prevail and be released. In hindsight, he regarded his imprisonment as a pivotal and formative life event that he would not choose to reverse if given the chance.

False hope can destroy

However, Stockdale clarified that maintaining this defiant conviction did not equate to simply living in naïve 'hope' of early release. He observed that the most optimistic of his fellow prisoners – those confidently clinging to the belief that freedom was just around the corner – tragically died in captivity. Stockdale recounts how these optimistic prisoners would repeatedly predict release by upcoming holidays, only to have their hopes dashed each time. The disappointment of clinging to false hope year after year ultimately destroyed them psychologically and emotionally.

So while Stockdale himself retained iron belief in his ultimate survival and liberation, he did not entertain fanciful optimism about any specific release date. His sense of certainty stemmed from an internal locus of control and self-reliance rather than wishfully pinning hopes on external factors outside his influence. This distinction proved vitally important.

What the optimists who lived in hope failed to do was confront the reality of their situation. They preferred to stick their heads in the sand and hope that the difficulties they endured would go away. In the short term, living in hope made it easier for them, but when they were eventually forced to face reality, it had become too much, and they literally died of a broken heart. Stockdale approached adversity with a very different mindset. He made a 'realistic appraisal of the situation', and acknowledged he was in hell and could not determine how long his ordeal would last. Accepting his dreadful predicament as reality empowered him to step up and do everything he could to lift the morale and prolong the lives of his fellow prisoners.

Realistic appraisal of reality

By accepting the hardships of prison life, Stockdale freed his mind to deal with his reality. Facing the bleakness of his situation, he was able to innovate in the face of tremendous adversity. He created a tapping code so he and the other prisoners, often held in solitary confinement, could communicate. He also developed a milestone system that helped him and his fellow prisoner deal with the damaging emotional consequences of the torture they endured. He even sent vital intelligence information to his wife, hidden in the seemingly innocent letters he wrote to her.

All these decades later, Admiral Stockdale's mindset is known and highly regarded as the Stockdale Paradox. It means that even though he retained faith that he would prevail in the end, come what may, at the same time, he knew it was crucial to confront the most brutal facts of his reality, whatever they might be.

The Stockdale Paradox remains a popular way to illustrate the value of *realistic appraisal of reality* in international management training settings and as a crucial lesson in self-help and personal development. At its heart, it is a lesson in resilience: Never doubt that you can achieve your goals, no matter the hardships. However, don't fool yourself or lie to yourself by just hoping things will improve. Make a realistic appraisal of your current situation. It is then and only then that you can free your mind to create solutions and strategies to improve your lot effectively.

Worksheet 7: Strategy focus

Use this worksheet or your notebook to handwrite the strategies that resonate most with you and you think will help create the most powerful changes in how you think and feel about yourself.

Key points to consider are:

- Was there a time, or a part of your life, when you felt able to deal with your life challenges? Look back on your timeline for insights or add events and memories on this theme.
- Are there things in your life you were just 'hoping' would improve that you could now address with the Stockdale paradox mindset?
- Practise checking in with your intuition and listening, to trust your gut instincts.
- What strategies do you need to focus on – such as healthy boundaries, increased self-compassion, managing stress effectively – and what can you start with now? Formulate your own daily practice from these strategies to focus on building your resilience.

8. Emotional Freedom Technique (EFT)

The Emotional Freedom Technique (EFT), or 'Tapping' as it is also known, is an evidence-based therapy approach created by Gary Craig.[11]

Having been around for over 30 years, it is the most influential and best-known internationally of all the Meridian Energy Therapies, a loose collection of therapeutic approaches based on the belief that the cause of all negative emotions is a disruption in the body's energy system. Since its inception, EFT has undergone over 100 research studies into its efficacy.[12] It has been studied with a wide variety of different types of people and situations, from helping with extreme anger management in children and young people; to easing the emotional challenges of chemotherapy for cancer patients and, most notably, for returning military veterans suffering from the effects of PTSD (post-traumatic stress disorder) and other psychological symptoms of distress.

EFT was one of the first modalities I learnt as a therapist, and I have introduced this technique to thousands of clients over many years in practice. I realise it can look a bit odd at first. As I demonstrate EFT, I am often initially met with a client's raised eyebrow and more than a tad of scepticism. Still, I don't mind, as I know how powerful the technique can be for creating insights, a-ha moments and the release of long-held emotional anguish. Technically, EFT combines elements of exposure, cognitive therapy and stimulation of acupressure points using one's fingers to tap on some predetermined places on the face and upper body (see pages 94-95). What that means in practice is that you focus on your feelings about a specific issue that is bothering you, then either say out loud or silently to yourself a short reminder phrase about the issue you are focusing on while tapping with two fingers on specific points.

When undertaking self-guided work, it is crucial to protect your mental wellbeing above all else. With this in mind, initially apply EFT to resolve and release minor, less emotionally loaded issues. Avoid feeling overwhelmed by addressing powerful, more daunting emotions attached to past events by breaking them down into manageable aspects. An example of breaking an issue
[Cont'd on page 96]

How to practise EFT or 'Tapping'

Set a number before you begin tapping to assess the emotional intensity attached to whatever issue you are addressing on this occasion. If zero is no emotion and 10 is the highest level of emotion, then what is the number? Take a guess; your intuition will guide you.

The set up

The set up takes place while either rubbing on the sore spot or by tapping the fingers of one hand against the Karate Chop side of the other hand and saying 'Even though I have this [insert problem or feeling here] I completely and fully love and accept myself and forgive myself'.

Repeat the set up three times.

Tapping

Begin Tapping using the index and middle fingers together of your dominant hand, tapping for seven or eight times on each Meridian point listed below and shown on the diagram, before moving on. There is no need to count and tap with enough pressure to feel a slight bounce.

Repeat a reminder phrase as you tap around the Meridian Points e.g. 'this chocolate craving'; 'this sadness'; 'this emptiness'; 'this anger in my belly'.

The Meridian points are:

1. **EB** At the inner end of one eyebrow, level with the top of the nose
2. **SE** Side of the eye, at the end of eyebrow
3. **UE** Under the eye, on the curved bone of the eye socket
4. **N** In the dip under the nose
5. **C** In the dip under the lip on the chin
6. **CB** Around the collarbone using a soft fist
7. **RIBS** Fingers of both hands tapping on the rib cage at both sides of your trunk
8. **Under Arm** Side of the body, level with bra strap or man's nipple with a flat hand
9. **Wrists** Tapping inside of wrists together
10. **Top of head** Tapping around with a flat hand

After a Tapping round

After a Tapping round, take a deep breath with a slow exhalation. Sip some water. Good hydration is vital with all energy work.

Check your number. Has your level of emotion gone up or down? Have other things come to mind?

You may well need to tap again or use any new insights to guide your next Tapping rounds.

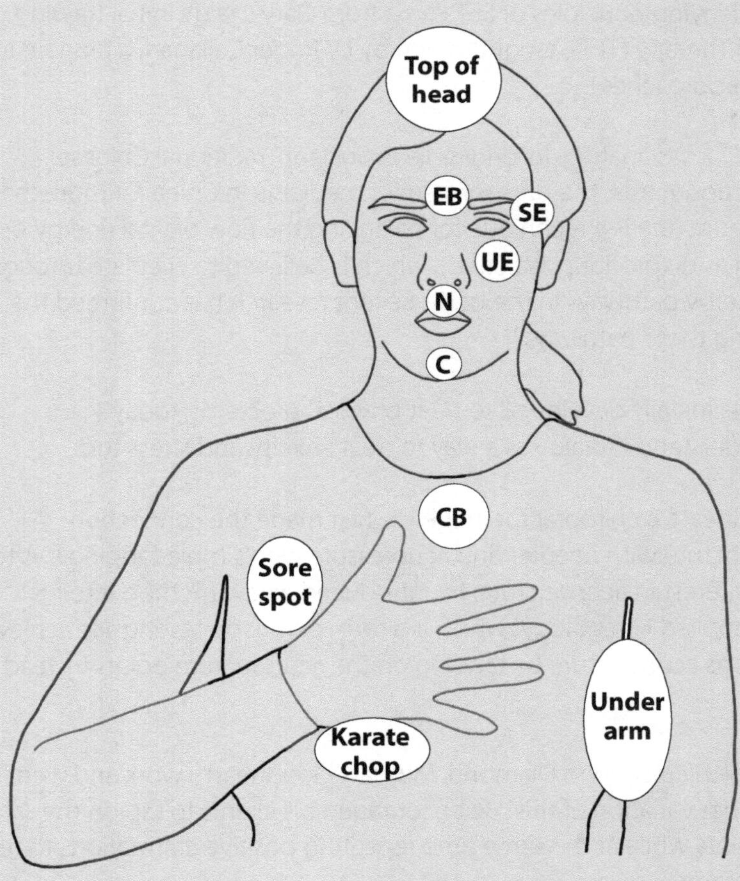

[Cont'd from page 93]

down is identifying specific feelings, thoughts and behaviours associated with the problem. Then, focus on one part at a time and reduce the emotional pain attached to whatever aspect you are working with before moving on to another topic. Use a notebook that you can dedicate to processing how you think and feel as emotions tied to events from your past become obvious to you.

The origins of EFT

Many of the underlying principles of EFT came from Gary Craig's initial training in Thought Field Therapy (TFT), taught to him by Dr Roger Callahan, a pioneer in Energy Therapy approaches.[12]

The history of EFT is fascinating. Its origins lie in ancient Traditional Chinese Medicine and acupuncture, the primary form of medicine in China for more than 5000 years. Acupuncture is a technique for balancing the flow of vital energy or life force, known as qi (pronounced 'chee'), which is believed to circulate through 'meridians' or energy pathways in the body. Recent research has confirmed the energy flow along these pathways.[13]

Acupuncture was initially developed to treat physical problems; today's practitioners understand its value as a way to treat anxiety and stress too.

Dr George Goodheart, a chiropractor in the US, first made the connection between acupuncture with needles and acupressure with simple tapping.[14] After developing an interest in acupuncture, he introduced a new method into his practice called 'applied kinesiology', which is a form of muscle testing. He achieved the same results as acupuncture by tapping on the acupuncture points instead of using needles.

An Australian psychiatrist, John Diamond, MD, saw Goodheart's work and went on to develop another variation of this. He encouraged his clients to tap on the same acupuncture points while at the same time repeating positive affirmations to treat emotional symptoms.

Dr Roger Callahan built on the foundation of this previous work to develop his TFT approach. He researched and created a set of dedicated, complex tapping algorithms or patterns, each designed to be the most effective tapping sequence for releasing specific anxieties or phobias. Callahan believed through his findings that, if a client concentrated on a problem or phobia while at the same time following a specific physical tapping pattern, then the issue could be released and, in some cases, permanently resolved. His TFT process was the earliest recognisable form of Meridian Energy therapies.

Although his development was revolutionary, TFT was complex to learn and exact in its execution. It was only later that Gary Craig, a one-time student of Callahan's, went on to develop a single algorithm or pattern of tapping. Simplifying the technique to a tapping sequence that could be applied to whatever emotional issue meant it was immediately more accessible. The one-time student had surpassed his teacher and developed his individual, single 'Try it on everything' algorithm, which he called Emotional Freedom Technique (EFT).

EFT as a powerful self-help tool

Today, I rarely work with a client exclusively with EFT. However, I value this approach as a gateway therapy to help shift clients from their analytical left-brain thinking into their more intuitive, emotionally connected right-brain way of thinking. This shift is essential as I often see clients who put more value on their ability to consider and solve problems logically. They're most likely great at their jobs, but that is not the mindset I need for people to access when they are in a therapy session. All 'knowing' and 'thinking' that goes on with left-brain intellectual cognition can be a barrier to where they need to be to benefit from therapy.

EFT elegantly and quickly pivots how people think about something to how they feel. And that something encompasses a wide range of issues, including fears, anxieties, phobias and PTSD (post-traumatic stress disorder), as well as physical problems around disordered eating through the management and reduction of pain. For this, I want the client to be open to how they feel about the issues they're dealing with instead of just how they think about them.

The crucial place EFT continues to occupy for me in my therapy practice, and I really can't see this changing, is as a powerful and easy-to-use self-help tool. I feel it is part of my responsibility as an ethical therapist to teach EFT to my clients. I want to equip people with a tool for life that they can independently apply whenever they need to clear negativity or when feeling buffeted and overwhelmed by life's challenges. Using EFT on self-identified issues means you can gain clarity and feel grounded and safe.

It's not necessary to overthink EFT, although I know plenty of clients who've tried to. It is easy enough to learn. It can be mastered by most people, including quite young children who love it. Also, you don't have to believe in Meridians or energy therapy for it to work.

Note: In the resources section at the rear of this book, you can access a link to download a printer-friendly EFT *aide memoir* pdf and a link to watch an easy-to-follow video demonstration of EFT.

Working successfully with EFT

You will need to be sure you have some privacy and will not be disturbed for at least 20 minutes. Turn off your phone. Have a glass of water to hand and a notebook and a pen. When you use EFT within a therapy session, the therapist helps you to get to the core issues you need to work on. They may do that by asking questions or just listening and bearing witness to you. Often it can be what a client doesn't say, when they pause to take a breath, or when their emotions break through, which provides clues to where the therapy work needs to be directed.

When you're working on your own, there are some simple guidelines to being a detective of your psychology.

Here are some approaches you can use to focus your EFT work that can reveal to you some of the dynamics you may not have been fully aware of.

Letting go of limiting beliefs

Limiting beliefs are often unspoken thoughts you accept without testing whether they are true. These thoughts are rarely shared or see the light of day, existing as they do in the shadowlands of your conscious mind. They remain untested and taken for the truth, even though they are often untrue. What limiting beliefs do, though, is keep you in your place. They stop you from attempting to achieve your goals or encourage sub-conscious self-sabotaging behaviour to ensure you never do so.

Limiting beliefs are a rich seam to explore with EFT. I frequently hear the following examples from clients struggling with resilience.

- I'll never make anything of myself.
- I'm never the most important person to anyone else.
- I am disposable.
- My friends won't like me if they find out what I'm really like.
- If I step up, then maybe I'll fail.
- It is hard to value myself when those in my family never value me.

Write your limiting beliefs in a notebook or on the next worksheet to bring them into the light. Acknowledging them and perhaps noting any insights into where they originated is vital in releasing beliefs that hold you back and stop you from fulfilling your full potential. As you compile your list, tap with a soft fist on your collarbone to help you tune into your unspoken limiting beliefs about yourself. Allow yourself to feel the frustration of how these beliefs are stumbling blocks in the way of the successful life you want to lead.

Give yourself plenty of time to get in touch with your limiting beliefs. Do not expect them to be realistic, sensible or logical. Don't judge or edit them. Write down as many as you can. Hearing and acknowledging them is the first step to recognising them for the unhelpful thoughts they are. Each time you note down one of your limiting beliefs, give it a 'subjective unit of discomfort' (SUD) number from zero to 10. Zero equals 'I don't believe that at all', and 10 is equal to 'I believe it strongly'.

This preparation shows you where you need to focus your self-help work using

EFT to dismantle your limiting beliefs and set yourself free to step into your power. Start with your thoughts that have a higher SUD score. As you tap around, say the limiting belief you are focused on in your mind or out loud. Don't become distracted but be open to other associated thoughts popping into your conscious mind. The goal is to explore the aspects of your belief and to look for proof that your idea is true or not accurate.

When tapping, explore how any of your limiting beliefs might benefit you, even if you initially think there are no advantages to having them. For instance, the limiting belief, 'I'll never make anything of myself', could be your way of never committing to achieving anything. The benefit of this belief is that when you don't commit, you never risk failing either.

Exploring specific issues

In your notebook or on the next worksheet (page 104), write down an issue that is bothering you at the top of a new page. Write your problem down in the first person, present tense. Here are a few examples.

- I cannot recover from being heartbroken.
- I am furious about how my mother treats me.
- I can't forgive myself for making that mistake.
- It's my fault for what happened to me as a child.
- Bullies always target me.

Once you've written down your issue, write as many statements as possible connected to the problem. Aim for at least 20. When you write them down, please continue to write them in the present tense, first person, so that they read in a similar way to the ones above but are aspects or additional parts related to the specific issue – for instance, 'This heartbreak reminds me of...' or 'I have all this anger in my body since... happened'. Don't get tied up by trying to make the statement's grammar perfect, as that's irrelevant. The important thing is to know the things you need to work on.

Use the SUD (subjective unit of discomfort) to scale your initial statement and all the aspects connected to it from zero to 10, with zero signifying no emotional discomfort and 10 being the worst feelings you can imagine.

As you become more adept and trust your intuition more, you'll be able to compose your EFT scripts, customised to your requirements naturally, and then you'll feel how powerful and life-changing EFT can be for you.

Reducing stress through deeper breathing

When demonstrating EFT to new clients, I focus on something with which they can quickly experience tangible changes and insights. Focusing on breathing works wonderfully for this, and I usually demonstrate EFT in this way. The full script for this is in the Appendix at the end of the book (page 131).

Awareness of the depth of your breathing to assess the level of stress you are experiencing is a handy way of checking in with yourself. When you are stressed, your breathing becomes more suppressed and shallow. Take three easy in-and-out breaths and make an intuitive guess as to the depth of your breath, with zero representing no breath in your body and 10 meaning breathing deeply, freely and fully. Refer to the tapping script now on page 94 and see if your breathing stays the same, increases or becomes more shallow.

Many people are surprised to find out how constricted their breathing is. Sadly, it's become the norm for them to unconsciously breathe in this way and therefore restrict the physical and psychological benefits of breathing fully and deeply. Breathing deeply and freely is a cornerstone of good health and wellbeing. EFT works powerfully and gently to free and expand your breathing from the straight-jacket of tension and stress.

Working without words with EFT

Some people get hung up about what to say when they tap around on the EFT points. Considering that a complete tapping round only takes about 30-40 seconds, there is no reason to be precious or overly concerned. Consider it just ad-libbing or stream of consciousness. There is no right or wrong way to say anything with EFT.

What is more crucial is to take your time to be present with your emotions. If you want to tap but feel stuck on what to say, it can feel beneficial to tap on each point long enough to take a gentle breath in and then breathe out before moving on to the next point.

EFT 9 Gamut procedure

This additional powerful member of the Meridian Energy therapies is valuable when releasing entrenched compulsive habits and behaviours. It can supercharge your results and be particularly effective if you find the issues you are tapping on are particularly stubborn or resistant to change.

And, if you thought EFT looked strange, then the 9 Gamut can look even more absurd, so it's worth taking a moment here to understand precisely why you are being asked to hum, count numbers and move your eyes in a particular way.

The EFT 9 Gamut procedure facilitates a bilateral stimulation of the brain. It works by combining nine individual activities that collectively take less than 10 seconds to perform. These activities alternately engage the right side of the brain, known in lay terms as the 'creative' part, and then the left side, known as the logical reasoning part.

Our eyes directly connect to the brain via the optic nerves. This process involves specific eye movements. The eye movements stimulate particular brain parts, including memory, internal dialogue and imagination. Other instructions include humming a musical refrain followed immediately by counting out loud numbers 1 to 5, switching brain activation from the right hemisphere to the left hemisphere, and back again. The full instructions for this protocol are part of the online resources itemised on page 135.

Worksheet 8: EFT primer

Use this worksheet or your notebook to compile a list of negative thoughts, limiting beliefs or conclusions you have already identified in previous sections.

Key points to consider are:

- With your list, score each entry using the SUD rating (subjective unit of discomfort). As you're learning to work with EFT begin with entries on your list that have a low SUD rating.
- As you use EFT more, you will grow in confidence of your ability until you eventually feel ready to apply EFT to aspects with a higher SUD rating.
- Remember you can add in the 9 Gamut sequence for extra support (see page 135).

Negative feeling/belief	SUD score

9. Hypnotherapy

Hypnotherapy is an excellent way of using hypnosis techniques to resolve various issues and problems, including relieving stress, managing pain and coping with childbirth. Hypnosis doesn't achieve anything of itself; it's what happens when you go into that beautiful, relaxed state that creates impressive results. It is an incredible experience, similar to daydreaming or meditation, where the mind is open to suggestion and the body is in a state of profound stillness, with no side effects or after effects. Despite popular myths, you cannot be made with hypnosis to do anything against your will or your moral and ethical standards.

Hypnosis is a state of focused attention and heightened receptivity to suggestions but you are always in total control. It is actually a natural phenomenon you experience many times during your day – for example, when watching a television programme or reading a good book, we naturally drift in and out of awareness. It is not sleeping, although you may drop off to sleep if you listen to hypnosis audio recordings when you're tired.

Think about the changes you want to make. For instance, you've probably succeeded in changing habits. Still, old behaviours eventually come back, and this may be because you have not addressed the underlying patterns that were causing your behaviour in the first place.

In hypnosis, you can easily let those patterns go and replace them with powerful, beneficial suggestions that fully support the new life you aspire to.

Hypnotherapy FAQs

What must I do before listening to the hypnosis audio tracks?

Find a quiet, safe place where you can relax without interruption. All the audio tracks are around 20 minutes long. Turn off the telephone, dim the lights or draw the curtains if possible.

Are there some people who can't be hypnotised?

No. It's a natural process. Anyone who can follow simple instructions can be hypnotised.

What if I go to sleep?

It's fine. If you doze off while listening to the hypnotherapy audio tracks, the positive suggestions will still go deeply into your subconscious mind, and changes can occur. Equally, if you are unexpectedly required to return to full conscious awareness while listening to the audio tracks, you will immediately be alert, fully awake, without grogginess.

What will it feel like?

There is no such thing as a hypnotised feeling. In hypnosis, you will feel the same as you would if you were engrossed in a book or absorbed in an exciting movie. It is a very relaxed feeling that most people genuinely enjoy and sometimes wish they didn't have to leave behind.

Will I lose control listening to the audio recordings?

No. You are always completely in control of your body and thoughts. Hypnosis is safe and has been used for a long time by dentists, doctors and psychotherapists. It is a proven therapeutic aid.

How does hypnosis help me to feel and think differently about myself?

When relaxed, your mind is much more receptive to the positive suggestions within the hypnosis recording. Your mind then goes on to make the desired changes you seek.

When you're listening to the audio, I encourage you to use the power of your imagination to embed all the positive changes you want for yourself.

Hypnotherapy MP3s included with this book

I have provided three specific, professionally recorded MP3 audios to assist you in building your resilience; the links for them are in the resources section on page 135. You can download these tracks to your computer or smartphone. At around 20 minutes or less, you can listen through headphones whenever you are relaxing. You can even listen to the recordings as an audio loop while you sleep at night. The hypnotic words will go deep into your subconscious mind and support all the positive changes you are making even while you are fast asleep!

1. Hypnosis to step into your power

Use the power of your mind to step into your power and own your value.

2. Hypnosis of letting go of the past

When building your resilience, it is helpful to let go of negative emotions linked to your past, especially those associated with memories and events or conclusions you've made about yourself that hold you back.

3. Hypnotic guided visualisation of your future self

Use the power of visualisation to see, and feel, yourself living the life you want. Please work with the power of your subconscious mind to find new and creative ways to make it happen for you.

Important warning

You should not listen to hypnosis audio tracks while driving a car or operating machinery.

Hypnotherapy pointers

Key pointers from this chapter are:

- Consistently listen to the hypnosis tracks daily to support desired changes for at least a couple of weeks.

- Know you remain in control of thoughts and actions when hypnotised.
- Identify specific changes you want before listening to hypnosis tracks.
- Notice benefits like stress relief and conscious insights.
- Alternate the tracks for maximum benefit.

10. The power of forgiving

Marianne Williamson is a highly respected American academic who, for over 35 years, has written and spoken about spiritual growth and personal transformation. Williamson has written over 13 books, including seven New York Times number-one bestsellers. She has stood in two US presidential campaigns for the Democrats on a ticket promoting the power of love to counter right-wing extremism. Throughout her work, Williamson has never doubted the power of love and forgiveness as the key to changing the world.

Forgiving your parents

She reminds us in her audio recordings on Forgiving Your Parents[15] that, for the most part, our parents did the best that they were able to do at that time with the knowledge and experience they had. She also reminds us that their need to be loved is as strong as yours. In adulthood, if you remain emotionally in a place of negative judgement against your parents, it can block you from experiencing your autonomy. It will separate you from any insights they can or could have offered you. It will also keep you feeling powerless and mired in a place of hurt and pain.

Resentment is a high-energy state which can feel exhausting to maintain over the years, or even decades, and can inhibit your spiritual growth. It requires an emotional commitment to keep the rejection of a parent or parents alive. These negative feelings are often fuelled by feeling aggrieved or angry. Feelings of entitlement sit unresolved together with feelings of disappointment and betrayal that can remain unresolved for decades.

Impossible to forgive?

Williamson continues by explaining that achieving personal awareness and maturity requires us to forgive our parents, regardless of our desires. Our mother is the initial and formative model of womanhood in our minds, while our father plays the same role in shaping our concept of manhood. If a man cannot relinquish resentment toward his mother, he will project guilt onto other women. If a woman does not forgive her mother, she will struggle with self-judgement as she grows up. Equally, if a woman fails to pardon her father, she will displace anger onto the men in her lives. And if a man holds onto grievances against his father, he will battle self-condemnation once he is an adult. Our parental relationships directly colour how we perceive ourselves and others according to gender as adults.

Williamson concludes by explaining that healing happens in the present, not the past. She makes clear we are not held back by the love we didn't receive in the past but by the love we're not giving in the present. So, how is forgiveness of our parents or other people possible when we feel deeply aggrieved by their actions?

Making peace with the past

Making peace with what has happened to you can be very hard. It might help to know that a complete narrative means it is not entirely about you. In his memoir, *I Never Said I Loved You*, journalist and actor Rhik Samadder addressed a letter to his childhood abuser.[16] He pointed out that he had learned some difficult truths about the man that harmed him that were challenging for him to accept. These insights created a shift in Samadder's perspective and showed that not everything is about him and his story. He recognised the trauma and adversity that led this man to act as he did. Samadder's making peace with the trauma he experienced revolved around his recognition that there is goodness and light within him so therefore he must also believe the same qualities exist within this man. As hard as it was, he felt he had to find a way to make peace with this fundamental truth in order to maintain his own sense of humanity.

You can either hold onto your grievances and anger towards your parents or others or strive to understand their limitations and shortcomings. This requires considering how they were raised, although it is essential to note that their background cannot entirely excuse their behaviour.

Forgiveness is not a path for everyone

Forgiving someone who has caused you pain does not translate to condoning or accepting their actions. Forgiveness is possible without agreeing to have contact with them, least of all being friends with the person who wronged you. Forgiveness entails comprehending the root cause of their behaviour. Through understanding comes compassion, not only for yourself but for the world.

The 'how-to' of forgiveness

An excellent method of forgiveness called Ho'oponopono originated in Hawaii and is rooted in ancient Polynesian mythology. In its Hawaiian incarnation, Ho'oponopono focuses on resolving family matters and the ability to right wrongs. It is a secular modality and has no particular cultural or religious associations. People use it as presented or modify it to fit their religious or cultural needs. Ho'oponopono is the practice of reconciliation and forgiveness that involves expressing remorse, gratitude and love and asking for forgiveness in order to heal and transform relationships. It asks us to heal it through forgiveness; through bringing our love to the situation, in the following four steps:

1. State your love for the person, place or thing you want to heal: 'I love you.'
2. Next, ask for forgiveness: 'Forgive me.'
3. Then apologise: 'I'm sorry.'
4. Finally, give thanks for the opportunity to heal: 'Thank you.'

When you say Ho'oponopono, it goes like this:

> Visualise the person, place or thing you want to feel better about and then say silently or aloud:
>
> 'I love you. Forgive me. I'm sorry. Thank you.'

And, like all mantras, you say it repetitively until it becomes a meditation on forgiveness.

This mantra can help transform many different parts of your life.

When I think about someone who has caused me great pain, I bring them to mind, send them love, and ask for forgiveness for holding onto negativity. I say I'm sorry, and allow myself a moment of gratitude for this opportunity to transform and move forward.

Use this mantra if you are in a ruminative negative thinking spiral about someone. Just say it and send Ho'oponopono to them. The focus may be on them, but it is you who can feel liberated when you let go of past hurt.

Worksheet 9: The list of unforgiven people

Use this worksheet or your notebook to handwrite the list of people you are currently refusing to forgive.

Key points to consider are:

- Score each person using the SUD (subjective unit of discomfort) approach, with zero meaning 'I can forgive them easily and effortlessly' and 10 representing their being unforgivable.
- Prepare to use EFT, beginning with some of the people on your list with a lower SUD score.
- Score the depth of your breathing, with zero being 'no breath in my body' and 10 being breathing deeply freely and fully.
- Tap on each of the EFT points reiterating why you refuse to forgive the person. Breathe.
- Tap another round saying their name and how much you refuse to forgive them. The SUD score can stay the same, increase or decrease.
- Keep going for a couple of more rounds of EFT until you feel a shift within you. Remember, forgiveness is never for them; it is for us – to free us.
- Check in with your breathing again and score the depth of your breathing as before. Even without fully forgiving the person you may notice you are breathing more deeply and freely.

11. The power of fierce gratitude

I won a runner's-up prize in a local village raffle. It was two tickets to see American Country Singer Gretchen Peters in concert at Snape Maltings in Suffolk. I didn't know anything about Gretchen's music, but having looked her up online, she had an enthusiastic fan base who heralded her as an inspired musician and poet.

There are worse ways to spend a Wednesday evening. Sitting in the sold-out auditorium listening to each song for the first time, I suppose some of my worst fears about country music equating with misery lyrics were proved right. Some of the inspirations for her songs were very dark and alluded to all sorts of family breakdowns, alcohol misuse, sexual abuse and even murder. Allowing for artistic licence, I just hoped as a therapist that she'd found help for herself or maybe just writing and singing her lyrics was therapy enough for her.

One of her songs, 'Say grace', was wonderful in its simplicity and resonated with me. The song wasn't religious in an orthodox way, but it was undoubtedly spiritual. It focused on forgiving oneself for mistakes, a primary tenet of mental wellbeing and emotional health.

In this song, Gretchen says that if life dictates that you have to start over again, then so be it. That spoke to me of optimism and hope even in the darkest times – when you've hit rock bottom and are unsure which way to turn. Most powerfully, the last two lines of the chorus are an invitation to 'Come inside, set yourself a place at the table and say grace'.

Grace, giving thanks, is the oldest form of prayer. You don't have to believe in a god on high to take a moment to thank the universe or some higher power for providing nourishment as you eat. It reminded me of several decades ago when I was newly divorced and a single parent with a confused and distressed five-year-old boy. Many people, myself included, have had to strive for the idea of home, of coming home.

We had lost a lot, and I wasn't sure we'd ever find our true home again, and I can recall how overwhelming that felt. I also know how peaceful it feels all this time later to acknowledge that I have found my way, and so has my son. Gratitude work is one of the most effective ways to increase your feelings of being grounded, and it's the perfect way to come home to yourself. I highly recommend it as an act of affirmation to include every day.

At the end of your day, preferably just before sleep, jot down in a notebook all the things that happened to you during the day that you are grateful for. The physical process of handwriting these is important, so no typing, please.

Recalling anything you feel thankful for can be difficult in demanding and challenging times. As you commit to this nightly process, more things will come into your thoughts, and eventually, they will more readily come to your mind. Psychologists have worked out that it takes 21 days to embed a new habit, so commit to your gratitude process for at least three weeks. You may find it so valuable to your mental wellbeing that you happily continue.

Recalling everything you feel grateful for will reap happiness for you in an almost magical way. Begin first with just a few things you are thankful for and try to increase these over several days into a list of 50 things you can express gratitude for.

To gain optimal benefits before you go to sleep, read through your list silently or aloud to yourself. While reading, you can tap with a soft fist around your collarbone, so you combine the power of your words with EFT. While you sleep soundly, your subconscious mind will focus on everything you are already grateful for and establish the ideal mindset to create similar experiences when you wake up the following day.

Compiling the list of things you are grateful for in your life is not a mild exercise, so don't settle for platitudes. American author and expert in gratitude, Pam Grout, first coined the phrase, 'Ferocious gratitude'.[17] What Grout meant by this was embracing an intense, fierce thankfulness – one that was forceful and confrontational rather than passive or saccharine. Rather than a gentle, mild gratitude, Grout called for an assertive, warrior-like thankfulness. She criticised superficial, feel-good expressions of gratitude as being too soft, weak or sentimental. Ultimately, she pushed for gratitude that was powerful, adamant and impossible to ignore. Grout implored her readers to express gratitude for even the challenges in their life, giving thanks for the demanding aspects. Being willing to focus on what is positive in your life gives your subconscious mind a break from running your habitual negative loop of dialogue in your mind – you know, the critical inner voice on page 51 that can be challenging to override, interrupt or change.

One of the most practical ways to transform how you think and feel about yourself is to change your thinking into thanking. Then express thanks and gratitude for everything. That includes the rain when you've left your coat at home, the blind date that didn't show up, and the job you didn't get. These are hardcore, for sure, and that's just the start. Gratitude can lift you from negativity by providing a portal into a different, liberating, uplifting mindset.

Here is a selection of reasonably generic gratitude statements to get you started. These are very general; yours will be more potent if you compose specific phrases pertinent to your life. The more 'ferocious' your gratitude statements are, the more transformative they will prove to be in attracting more of what you want to feel grateful for into your life.

- I am grateful for my life.
- I am grateful for all my experiences.
- I am grateful for my ability to choose how I respond to my life.
- I am grateful for the opportunity to change.
- I am grateful for my loved ones.
- I am grateful for this amazing planet and all the richness it offers me.
- I am grateful for my freedom.
- I am grateful I can change the way I feel.
- I am grateful for all the blessings I have received.
- I am grateful for my insights and learnings.
- I am grateful that my God is watching over me.
- I am grateful for all I have learnt so far.
- I am grateful for all the answers and help that have been given to me.
- I am grateful I am finding answers and that I am free to change.
- I am grateful for who I am now.

In some fierce gratitude work with my clients, 'ferocious gratitude' has been heartfelt expressed for bankruptcy, divorce and even cancer.

When we lose things we loved, invested in or cared about, there is an intensity of emotion or often a clarity of insight that we can be grateful for even amid the pain and anguish. My gratitude work includes the end of my first marriage, even though I didn't feel anything like gratitude then. Other sad losses are on my nightly gratitude list too.

These are the threads of gold in your life. I want you to start noticing and celebrating them with your nightly gratitude work. Try it. Devote yourself to finding what you can be grateful for, and you'll find things to feel thankful for everywhere.

Worksheet 10:
Fierce gratitude list

Use this worksheet or your notebook to handwrite your hardcore list of the things you are grateful for in your life.

Be courageous. Be bold. Leave no stone unturned. Shock yourself with what you can find gratitude for that is over, gone, survived.

Compose an initial list of at least 25 things/people/events.

Key points to consider are:

- Build gratitude daily, writing specific things you're grateful for.
- Increase your list over time, reading it aloud before sleep.
- Tap the EFT collarbone area while reading your gratitude list.
- Cultivate 'ferocious gratitude' for difficulties that spurred growth.
- Let gratitude powerfully lift you from negativity into an uplifted mindset.

12. Afterword: Your resilience journey

Developing self-awareness is key for building resilience. This comes from understanding your emotional reactions and what triggers unhelpful patterns. How you subconsciously respond to life's challenges greatly impacts your professional and personal success as we have seen throughout this book.

This book has provided insights into childhood origins influencing your thoughts and feelings about yourself. With clarity on your motivations, you can decide whether they serve you and if old family patterns inhibit your potential. Now you have experience of examining your own psychology, where do you go from here?

1. Commit to daily self-reflection: Keep a journal to increase self-awareness. Write freely and without judgement. A journal reveals patterns and brings clarity.
2. Listen to your body: Notice how emotions physically feel. Use EFT tapping to manage reactions. This builds self-knowledge.
3. Observe unhelpful thoughts: Recognise stories about your worth. Are they encouraging or critical? Challenge negative self-talk.
4. Seek external feedback: An objective perspective may assist in resolving limiting thinking styles.
5. Release judgement: Explore your beliefs without judgement. Discover their origin and let go of those holding you back.
6. Connect to your motivators: Your values, goals, passions and relationships can anchor you in adversity.
7. Make managing stress a priority: From nutrition to deep relaxation, self-care boosts resilience. Limit unhealthy coping behaviours.
8. Remember, change takes time: Have patience and celebrate small improvements. With regular effort, you will transform.

You now have powerful tools to build resilience from within. By applying what you've learned, you can:

- Regain confidence in yourself.
- Feel centered and purposeful.
- Skilfully manage life's challenges.
- Create healthy, supportive relationships.
- Trust your instincts and abilities.

Your journey begins with a single step. Start with self-compassion. Then progress through this book, integrating insights at your own pace.

Keep this book handy as an empowering reference. Highlight meaningful passages and techniques for regular review. Share it with others on their own resilience journey. Your future self is cheering you on, grateful you took these first steps.

My wish for you is clarity, courage and resilience! The work ahead will be rewarding.

References

1. University of Manchester. Half of children in England and Wales now born to unmarried pareients. 25 August 2022 www.manchester.ac.uk/discover/news/over-half-of-children-in-england-and-wales-now-born-to-unmarried-parents/ (accessed 18 December 2023)
2. Office of National Statistics. Births in England and Wales: 2022. www.ons.gov.uk/peoplepopulationandcommunity/birthsdeathsandmarriages/livebirths/bulletins/birthsummarytablesenglandandwales/2022 (accessed 18 December 2023)
3. Maslow AH. *A Theory of Human Motivation*. www.all-about–psychology.com; 2011
4. Winnicott DW, Rodman R. *Playing and Reality*. Routledge; 2005.
5. Watts T. *BWRT: A Professional Guide*. The Terence Watts BWRT Institute. 2012 www.bwrt.org/BWRT:_A_Professional_Guide.pdf (accessed 18 December 2023)
6. Rothblum ED. Affective, cognitive and behavioural differences between high and low procrastinators. *Journal of Counselling Psychology* 1986; 33: 387-394.
7. Flett GL. *Dimensions of perfectionism and procrastination. Procrastination and task avoidance: Theory, research and treatment*. New York: Plenum Press; 1995: pp 113-136.
8. House JS, Landis KR, Umberson D. Social relationships and health. *Science* 1988; 241(4865): 540-545.
9. Voss M, Leroy S, Spitzmuller M. Intuitive decision making: The role of affect, self-efficacy, and risk perception. *Journal of Managerial Psychology* 2017; 32(1): 18-34.
10. Sinclair M, Ashkanasy NM. Intuition: Myth or a decision-making tool? *Management Learning* 2005; 36(3): 353-370.
11. Bach D, Groesbeck G, Stapleton P, et al. Clinical EFT (Emotional Freedom Techniques) Improves Multiple Physiological Markers of Health. *J Evid Based Integr Med* 2019; 24: 2515690X18823691. doi: 10.1177/2515690X18823691 PMID: 3077745
12. Thought Field Therapy Center. Thought Field Therapy Articles & Research. www.tftcenter.com/thought-field-therapy-articles-research/ (accessed 18 December 2023)

13. Feinstein D. Energy psychology: Efficacy, speed. Mechanisms. *Explore* 2019; 15(5): 340-351. doi .10.1016/j.explore.2018.11.003
14. Gin RH, Green BN. George Goodheart, Jr, DC, and a history of applied kinesiology. *J Manipulative Physiol Ther* 1997; 20(5): 331-337. PMID: 9200049
15. Williamson M. *Forgiving Your Parents (A Course in Miracles)*. Harper Audio; 1994
16. Samadder R. *I Never Said I Loved You*. London, UK: Hodder Headline; 2019.
17. Grout P. *Thank and Grow Rich*. Hay House; 2016.

Appendices

How to manage stress with EFT

Here is the full script of how to use EFT to manage your stress by assessing the depth of your breathing. By following these instructions the goal is that you will be able to breathe more deeply, freely and fully and feel far less stressed.

There is a PDF *aide memoir* of EFT as part of the online resources to use with this book and a video demonstration too. Go to page 135 for the full list of resources.

EFT demonstrates how stress can affect your breathing

When demonstrating EFT to clients I have found it useful to begin by focusing on something where the client can tangibly, and pretty quickly, experience some changes. I have found that focusing on breathing works wonderfully for this. I have therefore included a set-up for this for you to practise with as you work with EFT for the first couple of times.

The depth of your breathing can be an accurate guide to the level of stress you carry in your body on an almost constant basis. Many clients are actually surprised when I ask them to take time to assess the depth of their breathing only to become aware that their breathing is very constricted or shallow. Sadly, it's become the norm for them unconsciously to breathe in this way and therefore restrict the physical and psychological benefits of breathing fully and deeply. Life-giving oxygen filling your lungs is a cornerstone of health and wellbeing. EFT works powerfully and gently to free and expand breathing from the stranglehold of tension and stress.

Stage 1: Establish your SUD (Subjective Unit of Discomfort) rating for your breathing

Rate your breathing capacity. You do this by taking three easy in and out breaths - nothing forced or exaggerated. Then take a guess to the depth of your breathing with zero signifying no breath in your body at all and ten meaning you are breathing deeply and freely.

Stage 2: EFT set-up for the first tapping round

Tap fingers on your hand as described for the set up above while saying out loud:

> *'Even though I'm only breathing at a number...[Say your breathing SUD rate here] and I'm not sure why I'm not breathing as fully as I can, I completely and fully love and accept myself.'*
>
> *'Even though my shallow breathing represents all sorts of stress that I don't even want to look at, I completely and fully love and accept myself as I am now.'*
>
> *'Even though my shallow breathing represents all the stress I am carrying in my body, I completely and fully love and accept myself without judgment.'*

After saying this, take three fairly deep and gentle breaths. Breathe in through the nose and softly out through the mouth. Again, don't use any force or pressure.

Now focus for a moment on your breathing and assess the depth of the breaths you have just taken.

Stage 3: First round of tapping for breathing

Say words approximating to the following, preferably out loud, as you tap on each meridian point:

EB: 'This shallow breathing'
SE: 'Stress in my body'
UE: 'I'm only breathing at a number... [say your breathing SUD rate here]'
N: 'This represents all kinds of stress I'm carrying'
C: 'I have this shallow breathing'
CB: 'I don't even want to know why'
RIBS: 'All sorts of stress in my body'
UA: 'I'm only breathing at a number... [say your breathing SUD rate here]'
W: 'It represents all the stress I'm carrying'
TH: 'I don't even want to know why'

Pause.
Take one easy, deep breath.

Stage 4: EFT set-up for the second tapping round

This time you should say something on the following lines, preferably out loud:

'Even though I still have this shallow breathing, I choose to breathe deeply and freely and I completely and fully love and accept myself.'

'Even though my shallow breathing represents all sorts of stress I'm carrying in my body, I completely and fully love and accept myself as I am now.'

'Even though I'm only breathing at a...[say your breathing SUD rate here], I choose to breathe out all this stress and allow my body to breathe deeply and freely and I completely and fully love and accept myself without judgment.'

Stage 5: Second round of tapping for breathing

This time, as you tap on the relevant meridian point, you should say:

EB: 'I choose to breathe deeply.'
SE: 'Releasing this stress from my body.'
UE: 'I ask my body to breathe deeply.'
N: 'Filling my lungs with life-giving oxygen.'
C: 'I choose to breathe deeply.'
CB: 'Releasing this stress from my body.'
RIBS: 'Breathing deeply.'
UA: 'Breathing out stress.'
W: 'Breathing in calmness.'
TH: 'Releasing stress from my body.'

Pause.
Take one easy, deep breath.
Assess your level of breathing and rate it again from zero to 10.

Stage 6: EFT set-up for third tapping round

This time, while tapping with two fingers as you tap around, you should say:

Even though I'm still only breathing at a...[say your SUD breathing rate here], I choose to breathe out stress and allow my body to breathe in calmness and I completely and fully love and accept myself.

Even though I am carrying all this stress in my body, I choose to allow myself to breathe deeply and fully and I completely and fully love and accept myself as I am now.

Even though my shallow breathing represents all sorts of stuff I don't even want to look at, I allow myself to breathe in calmness and breathe out tension.

Stage 7: Third round of tapping for breathing

In this third round the statements to make are:

EB: 'Releasing the remaining tightness from my breathing.'
SE: 'Releasing the remaining stress from my body.'
UE: 'Releasing more with every breath.'
N: 'Breathing deeper with every breath.'
C: 'Choosing to breathe deeply and easily.'
CB: 'Releasing the remaining stress from my body.'
RIBS: 'Breathing in forgiveness and peace.'
UA: 'Breathing out stress and tension.'
W: 'Allowing myself to breathe fully.'
TH: 'Filling my lungs with life-giving oxygen.'

Pause.
Take one easy, deep breath.
Assess your level of breathing and rate it from zero to 10.

Note: Repeat the first tapping round if required to further reduce your SUD rating.

Online resources to accompany this book

You can access some useful online resources to help you make the most of this book by going to:

https://workingonthebody.com/the-getting-of-resilience-resources/

You will find:

- EFT aide memoir
- PDF downloads of the worksheets for you to print out.
- Mp3 audio hypnosis downloads.
- Video demonstration of EFT.
- 9 Gamut point instructions.
- Blog posts on the theme of building resilience.
- Bonus additional information including video sequences and specially created explanations of therapy techniques.

How to contact the author

Sally Baker APAQAM
Award-winning Senior Therapist, Clinical Supervisor, author and speaker

Qualified Accredited Member of APA
Associate Therapist HAYA (Hunt Academy for Young Actors)
Orpheus Licensed Therapist
Diploma Hypnotherapy Dip PH (Distinction)
Advanced Certificate in Education (Canterbury Christ Church University)
Advanced Emotional Freedom Practitioner (EFT)
BWRT (Brain Wave Recursive Therapy)
Licensed Member of the General Hypnotherapy Register (GHR)
Member of Association of Meridian Therapies (AMT) London, England

sally@workingonthebody.com
www.workingonthebody.com
Tel: + (0) 7986 812851

Other titles by Sally Baker, co-authored with Liz Hogon, published By Hammersmith Health Books

7 Simple Steps to Stop Emotional Eating

How to Feel Differently About Food

Index

NOTES

NOTES

Also by Sally Baker, with Liz Hogon…

How to Feel Differently About Food

Liberation and recovery from emotional eating

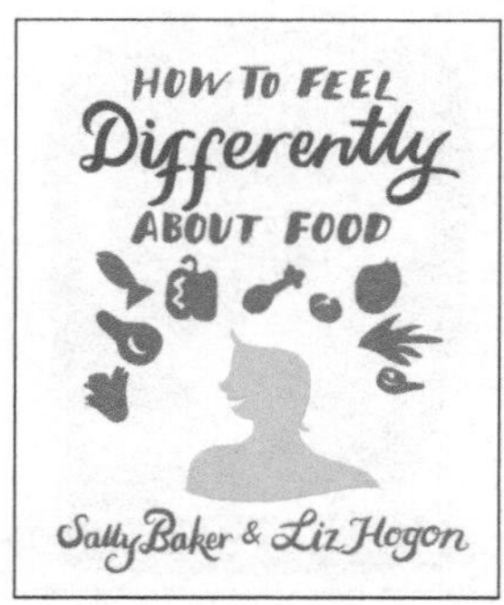

With nutritional guidance from Eve Gilmore

A practical guide to the relationship between food and mood - between what we eat and how we feel emotionally. This is the missing component in changing our relationship with food - we need to be getting the right fuel and not be creating cravings with a high-carb, high-processed diet.

Find out the best way to eat for:

- enhanced mood
- improved health
- greater energy
- stable blood sugar levels
- elimination of cravings.

Also by Sally Baker, with Liz Hogon...

Seven Simple Steps to Stop Emotional Eating

Targeting your body by changing your mind

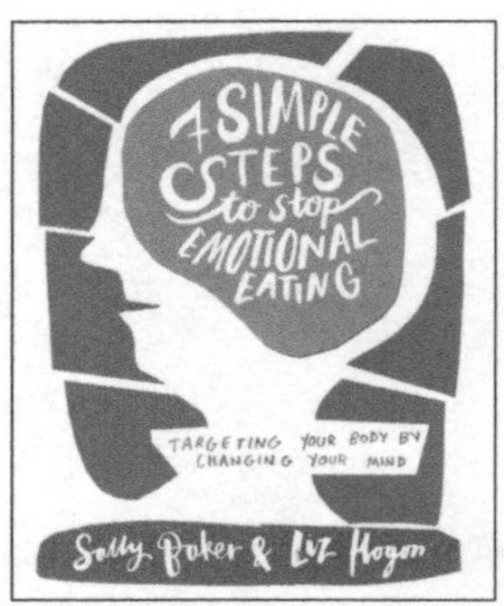

A practical guide to understanding and resolving the reasons for emotional and disordered eating, based on Sally and Liz's training and extensive experience in:

- Emotional freedom technique (EFT)
- Hypnotherapy
- and other related therapies.

With case histories, worksheets and step-by-step exercises integrated with free online materials.

www.workingonthebody.com/your7simplesteps/
www.hammersmithbooks.co.uk